Harvard Prize Book

Tʜᴇ PRIZE BOOK of the Harvard Alumni Association shall be awarded to the outstanding student in the next to the graduating class who "displays excellence in scholarship and high character, combined with achievement in other fields."

Tʜɪs Prize Book is offered in competition

by

The English Department

Name of Sponsor

and awarded to

Eleanor Benko

5/22/97

Date

Montgomery High

Name of School

COLLEGE IN A YARD

II

College in a Yard

II

EDITED BY DAVID ALOIAN

HARVARD UNIVERSITY

HARVARD ALUMNI ASSOCIATION

CAMBRIDGE, MASSACHUSETTS

Distributed by Harvard University Press

A Thanksgiving

Most of all, of course, thanks to the men and women who consented to write the essays that make up this collection. They have given their readers a magnificent gift upon the occasion of the 350th anniversary of the founding of Harvard College. Their reflections upon the college in the yard — some written in the late 1950's and published in the first *College in the Yard* and the others in the early 1980's and covering a century of Harvard's life under five Harvard Presidents — are insightful, humorous, loving, critical, and eloquent. The changes from the 1880's to the 1980's defy any easy generalizations. Each writer has given a view of the changing and unchanging Harvard.

Thanks are also due to Deane Lord, Lawrence Pratt '26, William Bentinck-Smith '37, and John H. Finley '25. The four of them participated in the difficult process of editing and selecting these essays. Deane Lord and Laurie Pratt, however, were more than co-editors; they were the catalysts who foresaw six years ago that this volume would be an excellent contribution to the 350th anniversary celebrations. Without their enthusiasm, this book would not have been published.

Special thanks are due to President Derek Bok for the "Introduction" that follows; to Vice-President Fred Glimp for his support and guidance; and to the Directors of the Harvard Alumni Association under whose imprimatur this collection is printed. While they made valuable contributions to this book, none of these individuals is responsible for its errors and lapses.

Finally, a word of thanks to David Ford, who has worked closely with me for the past eight months on the design features of this book, on the selection of illustrations from an excellent collection of drawings by Jack Frost, and on the arduous job of seeing the book through production.

January, 1986

David Aloian
Executive Director
Harvard Alumni Association

Introduction to College in a Yard II

The pages that follow contain the reflections of 65 alumni on the experiences they recall as students in Harvard College. The authors do not seek to describe their undergraduate years in a systematic way but to dwell on insights, personal examples, episodes and encounters that seem particularly memorable or especially characteristic of the College they remember.

The essays span one hundred years of undergraduate life, from 1886 until the present. This was a critical century for Harvard, a time in which the College changed far more than it had during the entire preceding 250 years. It was in this period that Harvard transformed itself from a small New England college into a large modern university.

This metamorphosis brought massive growth. The undergraduate student body increased from barely 1,000 to its present size of 6,500 men and women. The College faculty grew from 80 to almost 700. New buildings sprouted everywhere, and budgets rose a thousandfold.

More important than these figures are the changes that took place in the scope of functions and activities carried on at Harvard. The nineteenth-century college was a narrow, cramped institution with a curriculum that was largely prescribed and a dearth of extracurricular activities. Beginning with President Eliot, and continuing under his successors, came a long series of new programs and opportunities. Prescription gave way to free choice as the organizing principle of the curriculum, and elective courses multiplied. New subjects gradually developed: biochemistry, history of science, comparative literature, and many more. Intercollegiate athletics began to capture the enthusiasms of undergraduates, bringing ever more elaborate facilities in their wake. Extracurricular activities of all kinds steadily increased, along with services to help students study effectively, find better jobs, and cope with their psychological problems. With President Lowell came the House system; with President Conant, the joint instruction of men and women; with President Pusey, more scholarships and greater diversity of race and income within the student body. Throughout the century there emerged a succession of distinctive educational philosophies — President Eliot's completely elective system; Lowell's concept of breadth and depth (concentrations); Conant's General Education Program; and more recently, the Core Curriculm.

Impressive as these changes have been, extending into every corner of college life, they do not play a prominent part in the essays that follow. Instead, the themes that emerge are notable for their constancy. In this regard, the college years can be likened to a voyage of discovery. Although the details of the route may change, the essence of the quest remains unchanged. Along the way, certain kinds of recollections seem to stand out and give a lasting meaning: impressions of particular professors — not just of what they said but of the manner of people they were; friendships with fellow students; the special joys and problems of being independent at last; and, finally, an important insight, often prompted by some random event. These themes, running through the pages that follow, give a reassuring continuity to a century of almost constant change.

Another striking characteristic of these essays is how much alumni seem to emphasize the chance encounter rather than the planned intellectual experience conveyed through some well-crafted course or carefully designed curriculum. This realization is unnerving. Does it suggest that all the work that goes into preparing new courses and discussing new curricula is wasted? Hardly. The education that is planned, systematic, and orderly in nature prepares the ground to help students make more of their experience. But the moments of insight, the challenges, the examples that last are almost never planned. All that a college can do is to raise the odds of having such experiences by trying to fill the community with interesting people and cultural and intellectual opportunities of every kind. The effort to achieve this richness and diversity has been a constant preoccupation of all who labored for the College in the century just passed. The recollections that animate this volume are among the innumerable rewards.

Derek Bok

Contents

CONTENTS

THE LOWELL YEARS
1909–1933

CONTENTS

THE CONANT YEARS
1933–1953

CONTENTS

CONTENTS

THE PUSEY YEARS
1953–1971

CONTENTS

THE BOK YEARS
1971–

COLLEGE IN A YARD

II

THE ELIOT YEARS

1 8 6 9 – 1 9 0 9

JACK FROST

M . A . D E W O L F E   H O W E

In Gratitude to "Stubby" Child

During my two years at Harvard, where I received the degree of A. M. in 1888, I took all the courses I possibly could under Professor Francis James Child, accurately and affectionately known as "Stubby." Thus I made my first real acquaintance with Milton, Bacon, and especially Shakespeare, and also with a great teacher of long-continuing influence.

His pupils were aware that he was a great scholar, although not many of them knew in what particular field of English letters. It was only the other day, February 25, 1957, that the London *Times Literary Supplement* printed an enthusiastic review of a new edition of Child's "English and Scottish Popular Ballads," on which he was at work through much of his unbroken fifty years' teaching career. This *magnum opus*, completed with the help of his pupil and successor, George Lyman Kittredge, is hailed to-day as an enduring masterpiece of scholarship.

My relations with him had been only in the classroom. I remember no specific word of wisdom that fell from his lips. I do remember that he gave his Boeotian students an understanding of the distinction between *will* and *shall, should* and *would.* What is far more important, I learned to distinguish between the best and the less than that in writing, and, by a parallel scale of measurement, in men. In a word, I believe now that I formed under Child some of the standards of taste which I have long accepted as valid.

In this record of gratitude I must not forget to say that when my studies at Harvard were done Professor Child gave me a note of introduction to Horace E. Scudder, editor of the *Atlantic Monthly,* which led a few years later to my becoming his assistant editor.

Wordsworth may or may not have been right in saying that Shakespeare unlocked his heart with the key of sonnets. Nobody can question the fact that a gifted person unlocks his heart in familiar letters, not intended for publication. Thus, twice in my lifetime I have had a sort of recurring graduate course in Child, his work and his personality, his diversions and the objects of his devotion.

The first occasion came when my friend, the late Henry D. Sedgwick, proposed my making a book out of Professor Child's many letters to Miss Emily Tuckerman of Stockbridge and New York. This resulted in the publication of "A Scholar's Letters to a Young Lady," in a limited edition produced by the Atlantic Monthly Press in 1920.

The second occasion of dealing directly with Child came through my collaboration with G. W. Cottrell, Jr., of the Harvard College Library, in editing "The Scholar-Friends," (Harvard University Press 1952,) made up of the letters in the College Library that passed, from 1849 to 1891, between Child and James Russell Lowell, his beloved "Jamie." The book appeared more than six decades after I had "sat under" Child.

When the first occasion arose, I sought to supplement my very limited knowledge of the letter-writer by finding out what he meant to those who knew him best. I learned at once that his classmate, neighbor, and kinsman by marriage, Charles Eliot Norton, applied to him on his death a series of adjectives so truly apposite to Child that I revive them here: "Original, quaint, humorous, sweet, sympathetic, tender." I found that William James, another neighbor, had declared: "I *loved* Child more than any man I know." To me he had been chiefly the master under whose teaching I had unconsciously lived — the figure "all finely circular," as Henry James called him, who seemed never to justify more the sobriquet of Stubby than when seen, short, rotund, curly-headed, plodding across the Yard, his large, loose bag of books almost trailing on the ground.

When the editing of the letters to Miss Tuckerman was entrusted to me, it was made a firm condition that the identity of the Young Lady should not be revealed. Everything was done to fulfil this condition, but the secret was soon out. Through this book Child became known to its readers for his devotion to roses in his little garden—*peu de choses mais roses,* he used to say. Then there is his capacity for friendship and his drollery. One of his first letters is signed "Your loving F. C. [Father Confessor]." From that it was a short step to imagine himself indeed a Father Confessor, a secluded Cistercian monk who signed himself with crosses before and after his assumed name, †Fra C†, †Fra Cist. †, or †Fra Fra. †, expressing a lively smypathy with his correspondent's doings in the gay world, revealing himself most clearly when, for instance, he wrote: "Ah! what a world—with roses, sunrise and sunset, Shakespeare, Beethoven, brooks, mountains, birds, ballads—why can't it last? Why can't everybody have a good time?"

When the book appeared I found that my enthusiasm for the letters was shared. Of course it was all a matter of taste. One of Mr. Child's daughters told me in effect that her father was nowhere else so truly represented. Such an "epicure in letters" as Gamaliel Bradford declared: "I do not know of any American letters that are superior to these, if any equal." One dissenting voice was that of President Eliot, who deprecated what he called "the spectacle of a professor living happily with his family and writing in such lover-like terms to a young lady." When I suggested that this was merely a form of literary fooling, he replied, "I do not like that kind of literary fooling." Of course, President Eliot did not know that Child had written to James Russell Lowell in Spain, deploring the ascendency of the young chemists at Harvard. "Alas!" he wrote, "three brombenzylbromides in the place of the three old faculties."

It may well be that President Eliot's high opinion of Child's scholarship, his vocation, left no room for admiring all his avocations. He must have admired greatly Child's interest in local affairs, including politics, and his activities during the Civil War, in which the condition of his eyes prevented his taking a direct part. One of these activities was to prepare a little book of "War Songs for Freemen," some by himself, others by friends such as Holmes, Lowell, and Whittier. The soldiers are said actually to have sung the songs.

Nobody knows what President Eliot thought of the Fish-Ball operetta, "Il Pesceballo,"* made with the help of James Russell Lowell, out of Professor George Martin Lane's song of the Lone Fish-Ball, with which no bread was given. In 1862 the operetta was produced by amateurs twice in Cambridge, in 1864 twice in Boston, raising substantial sums for war causes.

It is hard not to say more about "Il Pesceballo," the correspondence with Lowell, and other expressions of Child's fascinating, broadly inclusive, mind and spirit. But one must stop somewhere. Let me add only this—many long lives have been passed in the living shadow of a great teacher. I question whether the experience of many has matched my own, in having the teacher and his influence become so vitally alive for an early pupil through the privately written word, and this at intervals of so many years. To have received all this initially from Harvard College makes me one of the most grateful of her sons.

Mark Antony DeWolfe Howe, Sr., received the A.B. degree from Harvard in 1887; A.M., 1888, Litt.D., 1954. He is well known for his many biographies of New England's and Harvard's worthies.

* See "Il Pesceballo" by M. A. DeWolfe Howe, New England Quarterly, June, 1950.

CHARLES HOPKINSON

Briggs Yelled with Hale

Why are my sensations and emotions on the afternoons of Commencement Day so difficult to describe? That afternoon for most of the years since my graduation in 1891 has been happy, interesting and sometimes full of beauty.

Because of the fact that I was born and grew up in Cambridge, Harvard has been always present in my consciousness. In the eighties and nineties my family knew or were intimate with many of the professors. Their characters and peculiarities were well known and provided many of the anecdotes of their lives. There was Professor Norton, whom I heard say in Fine Arts 4, "When I look down on you gentlemen I see in many of your cravats — a horseshoe. What more degrading symbol!" And Professor Briggs, seen going to his seat at Soldier's Field in company with the prominent Unitarian minister Edward Everett Hale, calling to a friend: "You see I'm at the game, to Yell with Hale."

The Yard was a pleasant place and Holworthy a favorite place in which to live. Lloyd Garrison, '88, writing a poem about it says of Class day:

> Here for hours have sat silent pairs clasping fingers
> Till the stars and the fairy-like lamps and the singers
> And the cool of the night and the elm trees and all
> Had made Heaven out of Harvard and Holworthy Hall.

The boys in Hollis had to get the water for their rooms from the College pump near by, and I often walked across from Weld to fill my kerosene can in Harvard Square where the movie theatre now stands. When the Princeton nine were in Cambridge, the Glee Club

7

gave them a concert on the steps of Matthews. The Yard was the centre of College, and of course bonfires were sometimes lighted there to celebrate victories.

It was inevitable that a boy of my bringing up should go to Harvard, and fortunately for me (who was no scholar) President Eliot's elective system was there. So that, unable to answer more than two questions in the History 1 examination, after drawing my bluebook full of sloops and schooners to please my yachting professor, I could work off the mark of E I received by taking next year, the "snap-course," Fine Arts 1, and receiving an A for my excellent paper.

Having spoken of President Eliot, I will now tell some of my experiences with him. He was an important part of my life since I was twelve years old. Three years before that he had married my aunt, and our families lived intimately together, especially in summer. He had the reputation in College in the earlier years of his presidency of being cold and distant in manner; but that was because he was so near-sighted that, as he walked (very erect) through the Yard, he could not recognize a student he might have been talking with the day before.

He was a very sensitive man, easily moved, but with a firm control over the expression of his emotions. When the parents of a student who had been expelled from College came to plead with him, he left the room to hide his tears. At a faculty meeting when some project near to his heart had been under discussion, he found the arms of his chair broken in his hands. He delighted in personal beauty and was disturbed that one of his grandsons whose nose was broken playing football was never restored to his normal looks. There was on half of his face an ugly purple birthmark, which he had to see every morning of his life as he looked in his mirror. He could not but be conscious of the way children looked at him on seeing him for the first time.

But we who knew and loved and admired him, while talking with him and feeling his noble personality, never noticed this blemish. In his youth he had been made conscious of it, and so led a somewhat solitary life, growing mature sooner than other boys. He also had responsibilities thrust upon him at an early age. I think that he believed youths of the college age might have more maturity than they actually had, and therefore would profit by the elective system which he installed in the College. Also, being a great believer in liberty, it was natural to him to give the students great freedom in their choice of studies. If a young man was foolish enough to waste his opportunities, so much the worse for him; but he wanted the fine, responsible young man of character to reap the greatest benefits by choosing well his college career.

He was not always tactful, but was very earnest in his ideas. An example of this was when, after a long-awaited victory over Yale in football, we went in a crowd to his house to greet him. He came to the door, and after congratulating us he said (admiring courage and persistence in endeavor): "How splendid that stand of the Yale eleven was at the last five-yard line."

He believed in giving responsibilities to boys who seemed capable, and so one of the proudest moments of my life was when he put me, at the age of fifteen, in command of his large sloop. To show how he believed in never interfering with the man in charge, I will tell of how, when he was very feeble in old age, I took him sailing with an elderly guest and some women and a child. Getting anxious when the wind seemed too heavy, I lowered the mainsail and turned for home, thereby spoiling his pleasant afternoon. After we were at the landing, he said: "I think I would have dropped the peak of the sail."

I like to see him again in my memory, standing in the sunlit Yard at the celebration given him on his ninetieth birthday. He said some thing like this: "People ask me to what I ascribe my successful achievement of ninety years. I believe I have always tried to keep a calm mind, expectant of Good."

This seems to me to be a proper ending to my scattered reminiscences and a good memory to keep of the wise and noble character of Charles W. Eliot.

Charles Hopkinson received the A.B. degree from Harvard in 1891. A portrait artist, he has painted such well known Harvard men as Presidents Eliot, Lowell, Conant and Pusey.

Eminent Men

What seems to me especially to stand out about my four years in Harvard College are those men with whom I came in contact. And first of these was Charles W. Eliot. In the years that followed, I have seen many eminent men; but were I asked to choose the most majestic and moving of all, it would be he. His voice seemed to come from some deep well of wisdom, gathered after a hearing of all sides, firmly possessed, but open to all who chose to seek it. He gave you a sense of your inadequacy when you realized that so well based, yet tolerant, an attitude was beyond your powers; but he convinced you that so far as lay in you the best of human endeavors was the search for truth.

Next I particularly remember William James, Josiah Royce and George Santayana, for I spent more of my time in studying philosophy than anything else. Nothing could have been more fortunate to a boy, coming from a day school in a small city of another state. James was in the full flight of his powers. He had been a student of Wundt, one of the earliest physiological psychologists, and from him I, at any rate, got the enduring conviction of the parallelism of body and mind. To me it was always a contradiction that out of this came "The Will to Believe"; but his mind and his nature were so rich and varied that he was apparently able to harbor harmoniously what others with less gifts of conciliation found mutually rebellious. It always seemed to me that the angels must have visited his cradle and bestowed on him whatever was charming and understanding and helpful and beautiful.

Royce was a bird of another color. He too was as pure and undefiled a nature as there was; but his ways were just the opposite of James's. The one trusted to the authentic revelations of the Spirit; the other to the inescapable progress of Reason. Royce was prepared to defend all his fundamental propositions with an ineluctable logic that caught you in its coils and was intended almost to extort acquiescence. Later, as I looked back, it sometimes seemed that the outcome, quite unconsciously to him, was foreordained, and that he was from the outset committed to emerge with the elements of a comforting, though not wholly comfortable, Deism.

Santayana to us was the very essence of detached Clarity; he assumed nothing, was commanded by no one and brought to all questions a serene and kindly willingness to accept the answers with devastating impartiality. True, he seemed a bit too self-sufficient to need support from without, and one would never presume upon any familiarities; but there was always accessible a store of friendly helpfulness on which one knew one could draw without reserve.

These were by no means the only men from whom I got the leads that I have tried to follow ever since, at least in my better efforts. I feel towards them a debt that I have never repaid; but it is at least some satisfaction to be allowed to say once again that, at times anyway, I have tried to practice the faith I got from them: that faith by which only in proportion as we live in scrupulous adherence to the facts, as we can best guess them out, shall we justify our heritage.

Learned Hand received the degree of A.B. from Harvard in 1893; A.M., 1894; LL.B., 1896. After an illustrious career in jurisprudence, he retired from the U.S. Circuit Court in 1951, although he still heard cases at the U.S. Courthouse in New York for some time afterward.

The Right to Utter

In our time there are, as there always are in every era, elements in society that carry with them disintegrating influences. In our time I think the chief one is the development of mass thinking, the impact that it has upon the sense of responsibility of the individual which has always been a cherished belief in the Harvard tradition. The search for security is in reality a search for an escape from responsibility, and as President Kirk of Columbia said the other day, one of the most striking phenomena in modern America is this great growth of mass attitudes which generate the divisive influences which we recognize as intolerance and bigotry in certain parts of our country today. But it is the significance of Harvard that I have in mind.

William James had many sayings. My favorite one, because I sympathized with it, was that algebra, he thought, was a peculiarly low form of cunning. James had a saying that he used to repeat: "What is it that makes life significant?" I would like to paraphrase that: What is it that makes Harvard significant?

We have no monopoly on learning or brains or leadership or opportunities. There are many others that are our equals. But what is it about Harvard that is distinctive? What is the quality that men think of first in connection with Harvard?

I think it is the adherence over the centuries to that phase of the Puritan tradition which John Milton summed up when he said that the right to think and the right to utter — that is a quaint phrase, "the right to utter" — was the first condition of personal rectitude and national progress. To that tradition we have adhered. The shining moments of Harvard history can't be dug out of old catalogues, musty and going back as far as they may go. The shining moments of Harvard history have been the moments of sacrifice. But in our time, due to this mass thinking and mass communication that prevail at present, it has become peculiarly disagreeable, not to say difficult or impossible, for the individual to stand up against the tide of public opinion, expressed as it is in mass form with constant emphasis upon conformity.

In Harvard history it is the sacrifices that made Harvard. The transept of Memorial Hall is one memorial of extreme sacrifice, with those beautiful Latin mottoes 'way up near the roof that nobody ever reads, reciting that these men gave all to save the Republic — and the similar memorial in the Harvard Church. When I was a boy and we showed our family through that transept, or our friends, the boys always paused in front of the tablet for Robert Gould Shaw, and the boys took off their hats as they went by. In those far-off days which seem so unregenerate to many, boys did occasionally have glimpses into the sanctuaries of the heart that so enriched Harvard's life in past years.

But the golden moments, the moments that count, have been the moments when men did stand up. Back at the time of the Boston police strike, when Professor Harold Laski brashly made public utterances that offended nearly all of us, it was President Lowell who spoke out and defended academic freedom, defended Laski and prevented a demand for his resignation.

After the first World War, when Zechariah Chafee, who was the greatest liberal at Harvard in our day — and I use "liberal" there in the highest sense, the most sacred sense — brought out his book on freedom of speech, a committee of the alumni presented formal charges and asked that he be discharged because of certain statements that he made. A formal hearing was held, and who appeared at the hearing but President Lowell as chief counsel for Zechariah Chafee?

And so in the years when hysteria was growing in President Conant's time it was Conant who stood out in front and opposed the legislative attempts at restriction of utterance on the part of the teachers in the state.

And most dramatic of all was the appearance of President Pusey, when he with quiet courage stood out in defiance against the attacks made on the integrity of Harvard by politicians and evil-minded men.

To use Emerson's phrase, these are the incidents that we recall with "light in the memory" because they illuminate the Harvard history. The Puritan tradition of defending the freedom of the individual is a Harvard tradition. Those rights of the individual are frequently abused, and that makes their defense all the more difficult. But that is the price that we pay, and I submit that the significance of Harvard today in this country and throughout the world is derived from the fact that Harvard, generation after generation, has been and still is interested in defending the freedom of the individual and the right of free inquiry.

This subject has certain controversial aspects. But I think that we should all extend our gratitude to President Pusey and his associates, who have so loyally upheld this tradition in what David McCord calls "the most abrasive period of Harvard history," which has followed World War II. In all parts of the country it is the obligation of Harvard men to rally to the support of this tradition in all communities and on all occasions where the necessity arises.

Perhaps, if we do this, some of us may find that transcendent aim which Professor Whitehead emphasized as necessary to every life if it is to be made a life significant.

John Lord O'Brian received the A.B. degree from Harvard in 1896. He received the LL.B. from the University of Buffalo in 1898. Among his many public services he has been U.S. Attorney for the Western District of New York, Vice-Chairman of the New York State Reorganization of the Constitution in 1925–26 and General Counsel of the Office of Production Management in Washington from 1941 to '44. He was a member of the Board of Overseers from 1939 to 1945 and was president of the Alumni Association in 1945–46. He delivered the Godkin Lectures of 1955.

R O G E R I . L E E

Educating a Doctor

In the Fall of 1898, when I became a Freshman at Harvard College, I knew I wanted to be a doctor. I was somewhat mystified by having as my adviser a professor of Latin. The professor was mystified too, but said to me it was probably because doctors' prescriptions were usually written in Latin. So he advised me to take a course in Latin. He also advised me to take a course in Greek because he understood that Hippocrates, of whom I had never heard, was a famous Greek physician. Of course, I followed his advice. But I have never written prescriptions in Latin. And when I became a hero-worshipper of Hippocrates, I discovered that Hippocrates rebelled against the Academicians in their ivory towers, who argued as to how many angels could stand on the point of a needle. The rebel Hippocrates, besides being a great physician, originated a moral code for doctors, which to this day is the conscience of the medical profession.

When I entered Harvard College, I did not know another student. But time, of course, remedied that, albeit perhaps slowly. I had the great good fortune to form a friendship with John Haynes Holmes. Holmes wanted to be an Unitarian minister. We often disagreed, but our friendship held fast over the years. Holmes was a debater. I was a stutterer, and I envied him for his fluency. He was very musical, and he continued my musical education, which was begun by a school-mate, Harry Osgood, and was later carried on by another musical genius, a Junior Medical Associate, the late Bill Breed. My musical education, which resulted in my becoming a trustee of the Boston Symphony Orchestra and in an intimate association with such great musicians as Serge Koussevitzky, has been a very enduring satisfaction of my life.

I was fortunate enough, largely I suspect through the instrumentality of John Holmes, to be elected to a College club. The club had a table at Memorial Hall, where we ate. There the talk was more important than food. In the group were Frank Simonds, who made a specialty of knowing details of geography and history. He knew not only all the places mentioned in the Boer War, which was going on then, but any incidental place mentioned in the current news of the Middle East or Far East. When, later, World War I took place, he easily spoke with authority of the tangled geographical significance of many events and became justly a famous commentator. Also, in the group was John Macy, a gifted writer, who through his marriage had much to do with Helen Keller, the deaf and blind girl, who is doing so much for those who had the affliction of deafness or blindness or both. Walter Arensberg, even then a poet, was another member of the group. Perhaps the desire to participate in these animated conversations or perhaps the recognition of the futility of stuttering, largely cured me of my stuttering. In any event, I largely gave up the habit, although for some years I was sensitive to the contagiousness of stuttering.

In any event, in my junior year in College, I undertook to play the part of a female character in a play of one of Shakespeare's contemporaries. Professor George P. Baker coached these plays. We were all impressed with his contagious enthusiasm. Unfortunately, perhaps for me, the fulfillment of my histrionic effort was negatived by an attack of mumps.

During these undergraduate years, I came under the spell of Professor Charles T. Copeland, the unique character who lived in the Yard and who signaled with a light in his window if he was available to students. Copey did readings at times in a College Hall. His thesis, as he expressed it, was that if a student in Harvard College did not acquire the habit of reading good literature, he had wasted his time in coming to College.

I was steadfast in my fixed purpose of becoming a doctor. But I felt that the study of medicine resembled in many ways the taking of a veil for a number of years, and hence it was imperative that I should learn about such non-medical things as literature and art before I went to Medical School. I am quite sure that this view was regarded as a form of insanity by the College office and those who were my official advisers. I tried various courses in literature only to be thwarted, of course from my viewpoint, by the historical approach to the subject. Only in my last year, did I find Professor Barrett Wendell, who refused to take a Ph.D. in literature, and who later supported President Lowell in his plan of the Society of Fellows. Professor Wendell often introduced his lecture by saying that he did not give a damn when the poet under discussion was born or whether his parents were poor but proud. He said we could look that up if we were interested, but his concern was to make us appreciate the man's poetry and his use of words. That made a tremendous impression on my youthful mind. To this day, I have never been concerned about the statistical data of the great figures in medicine. My concern was exclusively their accomplishments.

Now I know that the story of an isolated student, who was going to be a doctor, is not of any importance. But what Harvard College is trying to do in the development of opportunities for all of its students is of real importance. To my mind, the achievements of Harvard College are not to be measured by the production of so-called scholars, who have been defined as those individuals who know more and more about less and less.

A few great intellects may require only the written word, but most of us need at least the stimulation of the spoken word in addition to the written word. Indeed, it is probable that more people really depend on the spoken word than the written word. Books cannot, for most people, supplant the lecture, the friendly talk or interview, in creating an education.

Harvard College is trying to furnish to all students the opportunities to come into close contact with great minds and thereby appreciate the richness of all forms of wisdom.

This, I take it, is the purpose of the development of the plan of the Houses and the other features of the Master Plan of Harvard College education. Thereby is opportunity for one and all, who are at all receptive, and is the basis of a true College education.

Roger I. Lee received the degree of A.B. from Harvard in 1902; M.D., 1905. He was the first Henry K. Oliver Professor of Hygiene at Harvard and acted as first Dean of the School of Public Health. He served as an Overseer of Harvard, 1930–31, and as a Fellow, 1924–53. He is author of "The Happy Life of a Doctor."

Nursery for Independence

The great virtue of Harvard, it has always seemed to me, is that it favors what David Reisman calls the "inner-directed" mind. This is an ungrammatical phrase, unless I am mistaken, and so is the phrase "other-directed," this writer's term for the opposite category. But everybody knows what these phrases mean, and everyone must be grateful to the creator of them. As I gather from "The Lonely Crowd," David Reisman feels that the "inner-directed" mind is dying out; and, if that should happen, heaven help all people like himself, thinkers, men of pure science, artists and writers.

But this mind will not die out if the Harvard way of life survives in a world of committee men, group thinkers and the kind of person who is described as the "organization man," the hero of so many modern institutions. In this world anyone who goes alone, walks by himself and fails to wear on his face a patent-leather smile is regarded as a menace and presumably a psychopath who ought to be subject to medical treatment. But how would any of the heroes of Plutarch, Vasari's lives or the lives of the saints have fared in this world in which only the adjustable and the adaptable have any value? None of these characters had any use for parties, crowds or gangs, for thinking in groups or in terms of organizations (as we understand these in our time), for the orthodoxy that is a touchstone now quite outside the religious sphere and is praised in every sphere of life. These men and their modern congeners are the "undisciplineables" of William James, and it is just they who have found at Harvard a "nursery for independent and lonely thinkers."

I am quoting James in "Memories and Studies," and I continue to quote that great and glorious human soul who made the mistake of preaching pragmatism. Why, William James asked, do the undisciplineables go to Harvard? "It is because they have heard of her persistently atomistic constitution, of her tolerance of exceptionality and eccentricity, of her devotion to the principles of individual vocation and choice. It is because you cannot make single one-ideaed regiments of her classes. It is because she cherishes so many vital ideals, yet makes a scale of value among them." (It is this making of the "scale of values" that has established metes and bounds for what might otherwise be a sterile eccentricity and anarchy.)

Could anything finer ever be said of any university? And does this not largely explain the noble contribution that Harvard has made to the life of the country and the world?

Van Wyck Brooks received the A.B. degree from Harvard in 1908. He is author of "The Ordeal of Mark Twain," "The Flowering of New England" and a series of books on the American Literary Tradition.

STUART CHASE

Working Capital

I would like to submit some evidence in support of Paul Buck's thesis about Harvard as a "torchbearer" to the nation and the world; the thesis he developed so eloquently at our recent writers' conference in Cambridge. The evidence seems to me no less valid for being discovered more or less accidentally.

It concerns Harvard's contributions, mostly original research, to our understanding of human nature and human relations, a field whose importance mounts as scientific and technical progress creates new and baffling social problems. My interest in this field is especially in economics, labor management, and communication, and I am constantly looking for dependable conclusions, backed if possible by laboratory findings, as material for my books and articles.

Listening to Mr. Buck, and talking later with Dr. Pusey, I realized for the first time how often I had turned to Harvard scholarship and research for this kind of material. I did not look for it there because I was a Harvard graduate, but because what I needed happened to be in Cambridge and nowhere else.

A partial list follows of what I have been finding at Harvard in the last few years:

First come the experiments of the late Elton Mayo of the Business School. He and his team of social scientists carried on exhaustive studies into what makes workers work, at the Hawthorne plant of the Western Electric Company. The findings have become a veritable classic in human relations, and have changed policy in factories and offices across the country, if not throughout the world.

I am proud to have helped spread the dramatic story of the girls assembling telephone relays at Hawthorne.

Wherever forward-looking managers are seriously concerned with improving relations with employees, they must turn sooner or later — and the sooner the better — to the research of Mayo, Roethlisberger, Selekman, Clinton Golden and others in the Business School. America leads the world in research of this kind, and it was the Harvard group more than any other who opened up the field, displacing hunches and rule of thumb by controlled experiments and careful observation.

Coming from the river to the Yard, I have spent many hours in the gloomy vaults of Emerson Hall, trying to find out what Messrs. Allport, Stouffer, Bales and their colleagues were up to in the Department of Social Relations — now dignified by the haughtier title of Behavioral Sciences. In Emerson one encounters research into group behavior, family problems, how children form habits, the nature of prejudice, rumor analysis, perception theory, psychosomatic problems. A recent report lists ninety-five projects. One day I watched a committee as it got into an argument building toward an emotional climax, while the staff took notes. The committee members did not see us, but we saw and heard them through Emerson's "one way window." (Yes, they knew they were being studied, but after five minutes it made no difference.)

Scientists at Emerson form a kind of super-department, which has led the way in combining psychologists, sociologists, anthropologists, and others into a single force attacking a tough problem. Academic partitions have been taken down. It is probable that most new knowledge in the social sciences will be found by teamwork of this kind.

The Russian Research Center, just off the Yard, was organized during the cold war for practical as well as academic purposes. It uses the technique of the "area study," developed in fighting the

Japanese in the Pacific. Whole teams of scientists were able to construct a detailed picture of what was going on in Leyte or the Japanese home islands without going there. While Clyde Kluckhohn was director of this research about Russia, he and his associates gave me much valuable material. The work of the Center bears importantly not only on Russian affairs, but on foreign trade, the performance of the United Nations, the rise of nationalism, on the whole grand complex of international relations.

In the field of economics, two men, to my personal knowledge, have made significant contributions to economic theory, something which does not happen every day. Wassily Leontief has developed what he calls Input-Output Analysis, where the output of every industry becomes the input of every other industry or institution. It combines economic statistics with double-entry accounting, electronic computers, and cool, hard logic. I believe it has a great future in explaining and predicting the behavior of highly industrialized societies.

John Kenneth Galbraith's hypothesis of "countervailing power" explains the relative equilibrium of the American economy since 1940 far better than any other theory extant. Five great power centers, he says, grinding against each other — Big Industry, Big Distribution, Big Labor, Big Government, Big Agriculture — have resulted in keeping us on a fairly even keel.

These cases are a small sample of the wealth to be found in minds and in laboratories at Cambridge. They indicate that Harvard has indeed been holding a torch aloft not only for wayfaring writers, but for the nation and the world.

Stuart Chase received the degree of S.B. from Harvard in 1910. A writer on the social sciences, he is author of "Men and Machines," "The Tyranny of Words," "The Power of Words" and other books and articles.

CLARENCE C. LITTLE
Teddy and the Bishop

Although I was born and reared scarcely five miles from Cambridge, was steeped in the vat of orthodox Bostonian tradition and was unfailingly secure in parental faith and loyalty, Harvard was, for me, literally a new world.

The sparks quickly provided by its great teachers of Biology — Parker, Castle and others — kindled in me an inexhaustible fire of enthusiasm for work in genetics based on an inherent love of animals. The precious chance to do research in that young science, even as an undergraduate, led happily and smoothly to graduate study and to my life work.

Students are frequently advised to undertake in college activities which they can use throughout life. Certainly the mice which I first met and adopted in Lawrence Hall in 1906, have produced in hundreds of thousands, by extremely natural processes, the continuing opportunity to do just that.

Again, when in August 1910, with my diploma barely "unrolled," Lawrence Lowell called me on the telephone to ask me to be Secretary to the Corporation, he opened the door to administrative educational work. From the outset he made the "room" which I then entered so charming by the warmth of his personality and by the inspiration of his intellect that, through all the years that have followed, I have never lost the contagious influence of the faith in youth which shone from him.

Among many amusing experiences of this era one stands out. It was a cordial meeting in the Union between Bishop Lawrence and President Theodore Roosevelt, a visting speaker. I was fortunate to be the student usher at the room where they met. After an almost paralyzing handclasp from Mr. Roosevelt, the bishop said, "Theodore, I am worried about you. You're working too hard and are too valuable a man to take risks with your health." Mr. Roosevelt flashed his famous smile, looked the bishop straight in the eye and replied, "William, they say the same about *you* and, you know, neither of us will do a damned thing about it."

There were, in those halcyon days, many unique and fascinating personalities who had, for me, the power of lasting impress. Henry Higginson on the Corporation, direct, outspoken and powerful; Dean Briggs that happy saint, all unawares; Terry, the loyal, human prototype of UNIVAC in the Recorder's office; Barrett Wendell, immaculate, witty and imperturbable; Bill Quinn, the lovable, competitive, untiring coach of field events–to name a few.

There was also extraordinary diversity and versatility among my own classmates. They have proved to be powerful influences on their generation: T.S. Eliot, John Reed, Walter Lippmann, Eliot Bacon, Robert Edmond Jones, Heywood Broun, Stuart Chase, Jim Sumner, Stanley Cobb, Francis Davis, George Martin, Morris LaCroix and scores of others.

Together, from the eternal wellspring of Harvard, each in his own way without fear or favor, absorbed the ideals, values and spiritual qualities to enable him to face his challenges and decisions, his successes and failures.

Harvard demands little or nothing for herself but she gives abundantly to all who will receive, the continuing and never-aging realization of the eternal nature of Veritas. This, as one moves through the years, becomes the most powerful and intimate source of love for the Greatest and Kindest from Whom the always wonderful experience of human life derives.

Clarence C. Little received the degree of A.B. from Harvard in 1910; S.M., Harvard Graduate School of Applied Science, 1912; Sc.D., 1914. He was a biologist and head of the Roscoe B. Jackson Memorial Laboratory, Bar Harbor, Maine.

THE LOWELL YEARS

1909 – 1933

Opening Some Windows

Who ever knows what college did for him? Looking back on my Harvard days, almost half a century ago, I find my memory clogged with trivia.

Freshman year I lived on the fifth floor of "Thayer middle," with showers on the third floor and toilets in the basement, a coal-grate fire for heating and oil lamps for lighting. Primitive? My father reminded me that when he was an undergraduate the only privies were in a row of sheds behind University Hall and water came from the Yard pump. Harvard changes!

Sophomore year, in steam-heated Weld, with baths and toilets on every floor, I made new discoveries. One was that an undergraduate could own a library. On the ground floor Jimmy Munn lived with his books. I seem to recall a thousand volumes. It was an inspiration. I went out and bought a few Everymans.

That was the year I took Philosophy Four, and learned, or at least experienced, what teaching can be. Those were the days when Harvard's philosophy department was unmatched in the world. William James had just retired, but Royce, Münsterberg and Santayana were still there, all brilliant lecturers. George Herbert Palmer, who gave "Phil 4," was never brilliant, but he was a magical teacher. In his quiet voice he would state a theory and make it seem important; then argue the opposite, and make that cogent. Thought was exciting in his classroom. I remember he converted me to determinism, then argued the case for free will. I lay awake nights thinking about it. I wrote a thesis that at the time seemed to me to settle the question definitively, and later presented it, for double duty, to fulfil the theme-requirements in an English course.

The English professor was so impressed that he wondered, aloud, if I had written it myself. Palmer had quietly excited me to be better than my normal self. That is the teacher's art.

Junior year memories are dominated by extra-curricular work as scoutmaster of Cambridge Troop Eight, Boy Scouts of America. We had a squatter's camp near the railroad in Cherry Brook, Weston, and I learned more from the Cambridgeport boys than from most of my professors that year. But I took Dean Briggs' English 5; and some of his gentle comments still rise to haunt me when I attempt to string words together on paper. He taught us the art of simplicity. He said that every time he met "meticulous" in a student theme, he had to look it up in the dictionary to be sure if the usage was correct; I have never used it since. I can still see the way Dean Briggs' face folded into wrinkles when he smiled.

President Lowell was installed, with exotic pomp, in the autumn of my freshman year; but the Harvard of the Class of 1913 was still President Eliot's College. We took what courses we wished; and my own choices seem strange to me today. I had gone to College intending to be a zoologist, and began with heavy doses of science. But five generations of New England parson-forebears haunted me. I soon shifted my concentration to philosophy, and before I graduated decided — so I thought — to be an economist. If one floundered about the classroom in President Eliot's Harvard, I am not sure that the floundering was a bad experience. It taught one something of the size of the universe.

Professors' homes meant more to me than classrooms—and whether such memories will be possible of the Harvard of today I wonder and doubt. At the home of Francis Greenwood Peabody, who presided over a curious department (called Social Ethics) halfway between Philosophy and Economics, I listened twice a month to the conversation of scholars. Dean Fenn of the Divinity School also kept open house on Sunday evenings; but what I remember best at his home were the Dean's readings from Mr. Dooley.

I took the privileges of Harvard for granted. Looking back, I seem to have been unpleasantly young, cantankerous, frivolously opinionated. I cannot say that Harvard cured me. What I think it did was to open windows, to glimpse remoter perspectives, to educate a little by preparing for the sobering discovery that, whatever one may learn in school and college, education is a process for which the longest, busiest life is too short.

Lewis Gannett received the A.B. from Harvard in 1913; A.M., 1915. From 1930 until 1958 he conducted the "Books and Things" column in the New York Herald-Tribune. His books include "Sweet Land" and "Cream Hill."

"Plus ça Change"

I am in a classroom in Sever, circa 1912, listening to Bliss Perry lecture on Comp. Lit. The details of that course have been largely forgotten, but I can never forget Bliss Perry. I think that what first won me to him was the fact that he looked more like an amiable business man than my then conception of a pedagogue. Feeling as I did about education in those early days, that did much to gain him favor in my eyes.

On this particular morning he read us a story. It was a translation from the Russian. I can't remember its name or its author, nor do they matter.

To hear Bliss Perry read was in itself an experience to be remembered, for he brought something more to the reading than mere diction. In some subtle way he conveyed to us, through his own magnificent critical sense, the exciting beauty of the written word. He made us feel that what he read was only a sample of riches still unmined and he left with many of us a desire to delve further and deeper which has never faded.

Similar revelations were turning up constantly during those years and in the most unexpected places. Rummaging about in the attic of memory I uncover a scene in some sort of a laboratory, a rather gloomy place with sloping walls and dormer windows. It is dissection day in Physiology I. The instructor reaches into a hogshead and comes up with two half frozen cats of distant demise. He hands one to me and one to my neighbor, with whom I share a bare wooden table.

"A fine specimen of Chicago alley pussy," he says, continuing to distribute the contents of the hogshead. "They flatten out a bit in the barrel, but if you lean on the breast bone they round out. And now, gentlemen, we are going to trace the circulatory system."

Restraining an impulse to be ill, I look on my victim with mixed revulsion and sympathy. I know little about cats, but it was obvious this one had not led the good life. Lighting a defensive cigar I make the first horrid incision. And then the cat is forgotten and the unpleasant odor (largely due to the cigar) goes unnoted as we trace the miraculous system of veins and arteries through the poor, half-starved bodies.

Now I am sitting in a lecture hall listening to Professor Kidder talk on Anthropology. To me these big introductory courses were the most stimulating experiences that Harvard offered, revealing as they did whole areas of human knowledge whose existence I had scarcely suspected. Under Kidder's magic touch Man's adventure on the planet Earth suddenly came into focus. Recorded history shrank to handkerchief size and the centuries rolled back into eons.

Or again it is Dean Briggs criticising a short story by one of the members of his class in English Composition. It was probably a terrible story, but the Dean treated it as if it had just won an Academy Award and his gentle, witty, but always incisive comments so impressed themselves on my usually sieve-like memory that I find myself frequently applying them today.

Now it is "Frisky" Merriman discoursing on medieval history to a classroom so crowded with "ringers" that they are standing on the deep window ledges, spellbound, while the rich pageantry of the Middle Ages lives again in that dingy room.

These men not only draw back the curtains on worlds of which we had been unaware, but through their rich personalities they created a lasting desire to explore them on our own, to find out what lay beyond the next bend.

When we talk about our allegiance to Harvard most of us refer to the Harvard which we knew as undergraduates.

We regard the present with the respect bestowed on things

obviously important, but imperfectly understood. Our affections, however, are reserved for the familiar past.

When I return to Cambridge I admire the impressive bulk of the "new" Widener Library and the graceful steeple of the "new" chapel piercing the blue sky like a knight's lance. I look in through the plate glass windows of the Lamont Library, like the little match girl, and envy the boys (they look like boys to me) who are privileged to work in such a setting.

But what really excites me as I round the corner of University Hall is the sight of old Holworthy where I spent my senior year. On occasion I sneak deferentially into the rooms which I used to occupy on the ground floor, hoping that their present tenants will not pop in and tackle me for a sneak-thief in the impetuous way of youth. I stick my head into my old bedroom, which does not seem to have been tidied up since I left it forty-three years ago and I try, somewhat mawkishly, to imagine myself lying in bed waiting for the clock in Memorial Tower to sound off the witching hour of eight-thirty before starting that ever sporting race to a nine o'clock.

Then I remember that there is no longer any clock on Memorial Tower or any tower either, for that matter, and I leave, trying to avoid the slightest appearance of sneaking, walking casually through the familiar Yard — here at least is something that has not changed. And at that moment I am forced to step off the path by two raincoated females who hurry past on their way to class.

Emerging onto Massachusetts Avenue I come face to face with none other than J. August, incorporated, that old Scylla and Charybdis on which my financial ship so frequently foundered And there, by heaven, is Leavitt & Pierce! It is difficult to repress a cry of pleasure. Can I believe my eyes? Isn't that one of the old brown Cake Box Mixture tins still in the window? I stick my head through the door but everyone seems to be busy, so I withdraw it and go my way.

Ah, the Lampoon Building, standing just where it should and

looking just as Lampoonish as ever! I try the door, but it is locked. Of course. It was always locked except on candidates' nights. It is only a few steps around the blunt end to see who is occupying the basement space. I am subconsciously disappointed not to find John's sign over the door.

At the River I come upon the magnificent and unfamiliar world of the Houses, the "New Houses" to me, although they are beginning to measure their age in decades and to take on the ivy-coated patina of passing years.

Once more I am a stranger in my own home town. But, as I walk the hard-surfaced paths which bisect the manicured lawns, the new and the unfamiliar begin to blend with the old and the familiar to become the amalgam Harvard — the same Harvard that occupied this ancient ground three hundred years ago — the same Harvard which will undoubtedly continue to occupy it three centuries hence — the Harvard which has never ceased to change since the day it was founded and yet has always remained distinctly and unmistakably Harvard.

Oliver Wendell Holmes probably once felt as I do today when, as an Old Grad, he returned to Cambridge. Undoubtedly he experienced the same pleasure as the discovery of an old, familiar spot and the same feeling of somewhat lonely strangeness in the face of the new. Emerson must have felt it and Owen Wister and Charles Francis Adams and Francis Parkman and James Russell Lowell and tens of thousands of others, great and near great and small. Almost all of them have stood on this ground, amidst different surroundings, and felt as I do now.

I have nothing in common with the Harvard of Holmes or Emerson or Adams or Parkman or, for that matter, with the Harvard of the boys hurrying past me in their baggy khaki trousers. Nor could any of these people have much in common with the Harvard that I knew in 1914. But these are merely superficial aspects. Underlying them is that intangible entity, a concept if you will, but none the less real because of it, which, through the centuries, has refused to compromise with truth or with freedom of thought and speech and which is dedicated to stimulating the intellectual interests of young men so that they will go forth and discover the miracle of life for themselves.

Perhaps this is what Harvard means to the Old Grad, but he will most certainly be embarrassed if you ask him.

Edward Streeter received the degree of A.B. from Harvard in 1914. He served as Vice-President of the Bank of New York for three decades. His books include "Dere Mable," a World War I classic, and "Father of the Bride."

New Bottle: Old Wine

I was five years old when I first gave serious thought to Harvard as an educational entity. My mother had brought me to Cambridge for a short visit to her mother who lived not far from Harvard Square, at that time an almost pastoral crossroads. The visit, I recall, had two unpleasant repercussions. One was that my mother had a sentimental portrait done of me by an artist on the pattern of Little Lord Fauntleroy. The other arose from my mother's taking me to call on friends, using the intricate system of trolley cars that abounded in Boston and Cambridge of that period. Late one afternoon as we moved up Massachusetts Avenue toward Harvard Square in one of these outmoded conveyances, I complained of feeling ill. My mother hastened with me to the rear platform and the conductor was both kind and solicitous.

"He must have been eating too much confectionery," he said.

My mother called this observation to my attention later. Only a Cambridge streetcar conductor would have used the word "confectionery," she told me. He must have learned it because of his frequent travels past Harvard Yard. Since that time I have lived fairly constantly in the shadow of Harvard University, and like the courteous conductor, I have acquired some of its tradition and a smattering of the culture it has to offer, more through osmosis, I am afraid, than through vigorous or intelligent effort. For instance, in my early childhood, my mother, whose family had attended Harvard for many generations, would tell stories of the Cambridge of her own childhood, including one of the Misses Palfrey who rode on tricycles with flounces around the wheels in order that their ankles might not be exposed; and about a member of the

Classics Department who kept a few hens in his attic. Cambridge, when I first became conscious of it, must still have had many small-town attributes, although it seemed a complicated place to me, even then. The "spreading chestnut tree" under which Mr. Long-fellow's blacksmith once toiled had disappeared, but there was a stone to mark its approximate site, and the Washington elm was still there with us in a deplorable condition of senility, but recognizable. Where plastic fronted stores now stand at the foot of Brattle Street, there was a fish market offering a window display of several enormous goldfish swimming peacefully in murky, greenish water gazing at the brisk horsedrawn traffic that moved among the trolley cars gathered at Harvard Square. Although the fish market has disappeared, I believe that the Billings and Stover drugstore was extant in those days, a young aggressive place with a soda fountain. I remember once when I was eight or nine, being given five cents by my grandmother and told that I might walk from Hilliard Street to Billings and Stover and buy for myself a sarsaparilla soda.

I believe it was on this journey, when I became lost and confused by Brattle and Mt. Auburn Streets and Massachusetts Avenue, that I first encountered a Harvard undergraduate. He was standing in the center of Harvard Square on a spot close to where the subway kiosks are now situated. He wore tweed knickerbockers, a Norfolk jacket and a visor cap. He was smoking a curved stem briar pipe which he had doubtless purchased at Leavitt and Pierce. He must have closely resembled the character in the drama, "Brown Of Harvard," a work which I wish might be given wider distribution. This Harvard man, who could not have been a Harvard Square student, was stately yet gracious. He took his pipe from his mouth — I am sure he was smoking Leavitt and Pierce Cakebox Mixture — and showed me the exact location of Billings and Stover. There were two other Harvard students at the soda fountain — I am sure they were, judging from this conversation. They were discussing the high price of a banana split which I believe was on sale for fifteen cents, and one of them made the following remark:

"I do not think in all my life," he said, "I'll have to bother about fifteen cents, because I'll always have it."

This attitude of affluence and indifference is still sharply etched on my memory. Those two young men of course must have come from that part of Auburn Street once known as "The Gold Coast" and I could already recognize the aptness of the name.

When I was a freshman at Harvard, Gore Hall, an interesting Gothic structure, had not yet been demolished to make way for the Widener Library; there were no freshman dormitories; the senior class lived in the Yard; the Boston subway had not been completed; the elective system had recently been replaced by Mr. Lowell's system of concentration and distribution; there were faculty and senior advisers, but no tutors and no Houses. Automobiles, especially those operated by students, were a comparative rarity, although it was growing obvious that the motor car was an increasingly popular mode of transportation. There was still a horse-drawn vehicle available to take students into town, but this already was assuming an archaic value of the Victorias now standing near the Hotel Plaza in New York.

There were great figures on the faculty. Professor Richards was working on the atomic dissociation theory; Charles T. Copeland was reading Kipling aloud to selected students in 15 Hollis Hall; Bliss Perry was lecturing on Comparative Literature; Professors Wendell, Kittredge and Briggs were in the English Department; the University was in a flourishing state. One was nevertheless aware in that era that Harvard was growing and changing. Without the dread Dutch Elm disease, the elms already were having a hard time existing in the Yard; pressures were growing to increase the student body. Fashions were somewhat archaic; everyone, for instance, wore white tie and tails and gloves to dances. Yet as I write these obvious facts, and even when I recall that drinking fountains for horses were extant and used when I was a Harvard undergraduate, I cannot feel that these days are as far distant as they actually are in the values of time.

It is true that two world wars and a stupendous financial depression have passed over Harvard since I was an undergraduate. It is true that social thought has undergone prodigious change and perhaps only a few people today would repeat the financial boast that I heard at Billings and Stover. Since those days, obviously, the industrial and physical changes, and the proliferations of Harvard University have been enormous and startling and new contingencies now arise more suddenly than was the custom once. Very suddenly indeed, Harvard appears to have become a co-educational institution. Almost within a decade the quiet streets of Cambridge have become jammed with parked cars, and the traffic around the Harvard Yard has changed from a problem to a threat, and the tower has gone — temporarily, at least — from Memorial Hall.

As I consider the disorderly montage of this reminiscent scroll, there is one aspect that surprises me and affords the only excuse for these recollections. This is that Harvard itself, as far as its tradition and spirit are concerned, seems to me to have changed very little from the day when I first ate too much confectionery. Any university must be inured to change, since change is the essence of its being. Each four years it welcomes a new college generation and it must keep in touch with youth, but then, perhaps youth itself is conservative. Harvard, however, never has been.

Combined with the sympathy of scholarship that has always existed there and is part of the democracy of learning, there have always been a tolerance and liberalism which have been Harvard's pride for generations and which have always victoriously persisted despite the reactionary efforts of splinter groups of its misguided and less mature alumni. In 1848, Edward Everett, in his capacity as President of Harvard, answering a protest against the admission of a Negro student named Beverly Williams, wrote as follows: "If this boy passes the examinations, he will be admitted; and if the white students choose to withdraw, all the income of the College will be devoted to his education." This quality of academic freedom, this scrupulous alertness to independence, had taken root in the Harvard Yard long before General Washington assumed command of the Revolutionary Army beneath the elm near the Common. Today its spirit still flourishes; it is in the very air one breathes at Harvard. Its essence is so familiar to anyone who has known the place that while it lasts, no one who has been a Harvard student or teacher can possibly return there as a stranger.

John P. Marquand received the A.B. degree from Harvard in 1915. He is author of many well-known novels, such as "The Late George Apley." "H. M. Pulham, Esq.," and "Point of No Return," some of which are related to Harvard. He served Harvard as a member of the Board of Overseers.

ROBERT CUTLER

The Coral Pig

Through forty-three years, I clearly recall one incident of the Yard, which has stuck like a fishhook. In that year, I was taking Charles Townsend Copeland's course in English Composition. I did very well in marks. But I never was close to, or liked or admired, Copey: — quite at variance from the popular line and from my attachment to Dean Briggs, Professor Neilson, and Professor Kittredge.

One day I went up to Hollis for a theme conference with Copey. He was sitting quietly in his familiar chair, dressed in a tweed suit, the sun flooding over him through the window and glinting on his spectacles. At that time, I wore on my watch chain my Phi Beta Kappa Key and a little coral pig given to me by my mother (symbol of a small undergraduate club of which I was a member). I was proud of them both: — proud of my hard work, of my scholastic standing, of the friendly society of my club, and of my athletic brothers who had preceded me in its membership.

Mr. Copeland gave me a long look as I came forward. Then he asked in his dry, astringent way (but not unkindly), looking at the coral pig on my watch chain: "Is that the emblem of your sublime little club?"

I remember each word as he spoke and my sudden flush of discomfort and distaste. I couldn't answer him them. But I could now, and wish my present duties in Washington gave me time adequately to write out the answer. Perhaps, however, I would not be as able to answer *now* if he had not asked the question *then*.

Robert Cutler received the degree of A.B. from Harvard in 1916, LL.B., 1922. After having been for many years President of the Old Colony Trust Company of Boston, he served the Eisenhower White House as consultant to the National Security Council.

The Cabots and Harvard

In the familiar verse that claims "the Cabots speak only to God," we are unjustly accused of snobbishness. I assure you, we listen to Harvard men other than Lowells. Yesterday, I lunched with an Adams and I have supped with a Bok. We do tend to take our closest friends from among the Ivy League types. We prefer renaissance men with a broad spectrum of interests. We admire the Rosovskys, the Kistiakowskys, the Wyzanskis, and the Vorenbergs as well as the Perkinses, the Homanses, the Forbeses, and the Saltonstalls. We enjoy our association with Harvard very much indeed. We like to be with the Atheneans, and we admire Spartans, too.

We do not go in much for pomp and regal trappings, and certainly not for sartorial splendor. It is achievement, not high society, that appeals to us. We are more at home in Boston than in New York. In summer, we wear dungarees, never white flannels, and can be found in Maine, not in East Hampton. There, we prefer North Haven to Islesboro, and are more often in Cutler than at Prout's Neck. We like books more than television, and I think most of us are more familiar with the works of Shakespeare than of Ellery Queen. If that means we are snobs, I plead guilty.

It is said that we have habits and customs, but no manners. This may be true, for we are a close family with many idiosyncrasies. We have produced a good many lions and perhaps a few jackals. As sheep, we hope not to be black. We try not to be catty. We certainly admire the cod more than the shark, the eel, or the jellyfish. And we tend to think Boston is the academic Hub of the Universe.

When I travel, and I do a lot, I am more proud of being identified as a Harvard man than as a Cabot. I love Harvard and the Harvard family of elite faculty, students, and graduates. I am glad that recent presidents have tried to broaden Harvard into a national institution, selecting its faculty and students from the best anywhere in the world.

Is it our loyalty to Harvard that indicts us for talking only to God? It is said that you can always tell a Harvard man but cannot tell him much. Maybe we are too arrogant, but I would deny that we are any more pompous than Yalies or Princetonians.

When we Cabots bleed, our blood runs red. I say, let Yale take the blue bloods and Harvard those red-blooded, hard-working, bright, and ambitious scholars who will protect our freedoms and provide the leadership for a better world tomorrow.

Thomas Cabot '19 is a former Overseer, former trustee of Radcliffe College, former head of the Cabot Corporation, fundraiser extraordinaire and nationally recognized sailor. Cabot House is named for Thomas and Virginia Cabot.

It's Not Anarchy

The Harvard I have known for over forty years seems to me, even in a time which the publicists like to complain is one of conformity, of "other-direction," of the "organization man," to be still almost an *abbaye de Thélème*. Harvard men distribute themselves along the full length of whatever curve of human behavior you choose to construct. We all know this and rejoice in the knowledge. We do not feel that this freedom, and this resulting variety, are dangerous to ourselves or to others. It is no anarchy.

For Harvard's multanimity, to speak only of things of the mind, has its own disciplinary value. No one, student or teacher, can surround himself wholly with yes-men and yes-things. The environment can deflate the very pride it has nourished. My own first deflation came with the first theme returned in English A; I can still remember that I had confused "recourse" with "resource," and what is worse, used "flaunt" to mean "flout." I think the instructor had commented on the whole essay as "derivative," and I know I received a stimulating freshman "D."

What stays most firmly in my mind as a fine chastening, however, goes back to my first years as a teacher. Among my seniors in 1924 was an able but not scholarly young man, who graduated with a safe "cum laude" — an honor I felt I had won as much as he had. He vanished, as seniors do, and turned up several years later in the Square. We recognized and greeted each other (Harvard men often do, in spite of the legend) and I asked the inevitable "What are you doing now?"

"Oh," he said, "I'm back at the Business School. You know, Mr.

Brinton," he went on very cheerfully, "I never really got much out of the College."

"And are you getting something out of the Business School?"

"I certainly am. We have the case method. We study *real* problems."

I had had him write me essays on topics such as "Had you been on the jury that tried Socrates, how would you have voted?" This I thought was a very real problem, even after 2,300 years, but clearly he had not thought so.

"How does it work out?" I asked politely.

"Well, take right now: I'm on my way to Central Square to study a problem. I'm a chainstore manager, say for a firm like Kresge. I've got to decide whether or not to open a soft-drink and lunch counter in our branch at Prospect and Mass. Avenue."

I hope I did not show my feelings. In that decade of Mencken and Sinclair Lewis we on the Cambridge side of the Charles were pretty contemptuous of the school that had just mushroomed up on the Allston side. My former student had found Socrates dull and a hypothetical chain store in Central Square interesting. So much the worse for him.

But I could not dodge the deflating facts: he hadn't "got much out of" me, and he had got a lot out of a kind of training I found — well, Sinclair Lewis had recently in "Babbitt" put it better than I could.

Now I will not pretend that this incident was for me a sudden conversion from intellectual snobbery to gentle but hard-headed realism. From it I do, however, date a slow process of changing convictions which has led me to two conclusions among many others: First, that my student was justified in finding in awareness of facing a problem, one not solved for him in advance, a major incentive to thinking and learning; it was up to me to make him see that history is full of problems worth trying to solve. Second, if after trying my best I were to fail with him and his likes in the future, I should not be hurt, but strengthened in my appreciation for Harvard's eternal variety. A Harvard wholly Irving Babbitt, with never a George Babbitt, would not be Harvard. Surely *Veritas* demands no less an admission?

Crane Brinton received the degree of A.B. from Harvard in 1919; Ph.D., Oxford, 1923. He became Professor of History at Harvard in 1942. His books include "Anatomy of Revolution" and "Ideas and Men."

P.S. to Dean Briggs

Looking back on it forty years later I find myself remembering the time I spent at Harvard as a period of afterglow. At nineteen and twenty I was mighty impatient with that afterglow. No more ungrateful brat ever ran for a nine o'clock across the old duckboards in the Yard. It was my fate to come in on the end of an era. Victorian scholarship had fulfilled its cycle. William James was dead. The afterglow of the great Transcendentalists had not quite faded from the Cambridge sky. Graduate students were still retailing awed anecdotes of Santayana. There had been a young poet named Tom Eliot, an explosive journalist named Jack Reed. They had moved out into the great world of hellroaring and confusion. I felt I'd come too late. Some of my undergraduate friends were trying to replace the ardors of the past with Oscar Wilde and Beardsley's illustrations and "The Hound of Heaven"; the mauve afterglow. I wasn't satisfied with any of it. I guess I wanted Periclean Athens right that day in the Harvard Yard.

It took me twenty years to discover that I did learn something at Harvard after all. Cambridge wasn't such a backwater as I'd thought. There was Robinson's Chaucer course, Henderson's History of Science. But it wasn't a question of scholarship: only years later did I begin to understand the uses of scholarship; it was the acquisition of a sort of an inheritance, — from "an age that is gone" just like in the song. Like for so many others, it was Dean Briggs who became the personification of that inheritance. Not that I appreciated him at the time. It wasn't that I didn't feel respect and affection for him as a man and, in the best sense of the word, a New Englander. The man was unashamedly himself. No one could help being moved by his lovely candor, his tenderhearted irony, the salty smalltown way he had of putting things.

But I thought of him as a museum piece, quaint, the way in these latter years we have come to admire American primitives; provincial. I was among his irreverent students who spoke of him as Aunt Betsy. Though we revelled in shocking him, we preferred most of the time to pretend that we were shielding him from the facts of life. What horrid little prigs undergraduates were in my day; I suppose they still are. In our idiot sophistication we thought of the dear Dean and his English 5 as hopelessly old-fashioned.

Of course he was. It's taken me a second twenty years to discover that his great value to me as a student was his old-fashionedness. He had an old-fashioned schoolmaster's concern for the neatness of the language, a Yankee zest for the shipshape phrase, an old-fashioned gentleman's concern for purity of morals, to use a properly old-fashioned expression, and a sharp nose for sham and pretense which was neither old nor newfashioned but eternally to the point. As a professor he was perfectly accessible. After I graduated I often regretted I didn't take more advantage of his open-heartedness.

The last time I saw him was in Paris in 1919, if I remember right, during the sham and fustian of the Peace Conference. He had been induced to come overseas on one of the fast proliferating commissions that were being posed to distract the public from Woodrow Wilson's failure to make the world as safe for democracy as we'd hoped. The Dean and Mrs. Briggs were housed, somewhat incongruously as it seemed to me, at the hotel du Quai Voltaire on the Left Bank. Who could imagine anyone less bohemian than Dean Briggs? I went to see them. As I remember I was still in uniform. The last time I'd seen him I'd been fretting and fuming because I was trapped in a backwater cut off from the main currents of life.

Well, in the three years that had passed since I'd turned in my last theme in English 5 I'd seen some life and a good deal of death.

War had turned out a great teacher. I'd lost all pretense of collegiate sophistication but I'd come out with a prime case of horrors. I had seen too many men die in agony. I had the horrors too about the kind of world the gentlemen at Versailles were arranging for us poor buck privates to live in. All through those years in College I'd been honing for "the real world." By the time I went to call on the Briggses at the Quai Voltaire I already had a belly full of it.

There's a special musty smell about old Paris hotels, a mildewed grandeur; after all Paris has so often been the capital of the world. At that moment it was again. I found Dean Briggs and Mrs. Briggs shivering under shawls as they hovered over an alcohol lamp that was heating water for tea. The highceilinged room with its spangled chandelier was wretchedly chilly from the raw breath of the Seine under the windows. I never saw two people who looked so out of place. Although they had both aged noticeably since I'd last seen them, they had a fresh rustic look that delighted me. The Dean's eyes were as bright as if he'd just stepped off a New Hampshire pasture. Mrs. Briggs' cheeks were *apple red.*

I've forgotten what we talked about — probably I was still shielding them from the facts of life — but I remember my delight in their country cousin look. Provincial, old-fashioned had become words of tenderness in my vocabulary. They were indeed travellers from another world. In wartime bombarded Paris of a few months before they wouldn't have seemed so out of place, but in the Paris of the Peace Conference they had the innocence of new born lambs. A soldier gets pretty sick of Mademoiselle from Armentières and all that sort of thing. Here was home, something more like home than anything I had ever known. I stayed on with them as long as I could. Too long I imagine. When I left to go out into the alluring treacherous streets of the city of light, to go out into the future, my future not theirs, a future where hope and disaster seemed about evenly matched and both seemed full of grime and bloodshed, I can still feel the wrench it took. I remember thinking, as I went down the stairs, that if it were possible to change lives with another man the way people do in the old Welsh stories, Dean Briggs even at seventy was a man I would change with. He seemed so much younger than I and, in a way, more enduring.

John Dos Passos received the degree of A.B. from Harvard in 1916. He has written many novels about American life — "Nineteen, Nineteen," "Manhattan Transfer," "The 42nd Parallel," and an historical work, "The Men Who Made the Nation."

Out of Oregon

It is after midnight toward the end of May, and the atmospherics are moist but fragrant. Outside my window in Wadsworth House a sudden rallying cry for Rinehart, like an impromptu Hyla chorus, has subsided. Examinations begin tomorrow: Lights burn late, and all the books of Lamont and Widener are piled together hopefully on the scale of justice. But nothing has changed, of course; and one little blue book still outweighs them all. In the morning the double smoke bush between my window and the south side of Grays will be infested with honey bees and Eight-spotted Foresters — the sunshine moth that feeds on our Boston ivy. The pair of oven birds and the redpolls of last year did not return this spring. The brown thrasher paused in transit as in the past, and now father robin has taken over. The Yard has a good supply of worms, but a few weeks ago he was making nothing but dry runs. For robins every day is examination day.

Forty years have passed since I first came to Harvard by way of progression through New York, New Jersey, Oregon, Iowa, and Pennsylvania: one long lariat loop that finally caught the now-vanished tower of Memorial Hall. I ask myself tonight: What was it brought me here, and why have I never gone away? These are questions easily answered in brief, but the second is unanswerable in detail. It was luck and pioneering in reverse. The Oregon trail begins in Boston, you remember. Parkman saw to that. It is a trail well blazed, and there are those who viewed it from the other terminus, much as a boy will look into the wrong end of a telescope. As to the anchorage: "Sir," said Congreve, somewhat ahead of Dr. Johnson: "I have the seeds of rhetorick and oratory in my head —

I have been at *Cambridge.*" Can such a notion have crossed the water? The late Charles Townsend Copeland, Boylston Professor of Rhetoric and Oratory, was never a seed-sower of that kind. God forbid! No, the attraction to settle lay in something of the spirit akin to what Thoreau used to find in his solitary woodland walk: a blend of inspiration and solace, of intangible reward, the unaccountable suggestion of personal accountability. Harvard is a clearing in the forest, a sanctuary of the mind, where the trees were felled in another century and where every pathway is familiar though it stretches almost immediately into the heart of the wilderness — Faustlike *ins Unbetretene.* Parkman, viewing the genesis of an Indian village, described it perfectly. "In contrast with the general confusion, a circle of old men and warriors sat in the midst, smoking in profound indifference and tranquility." That indifference, of course, is on the surface. For the tranquility, one has to strive. The words of a Nebraskan are also appropriate: "That is happiness," says Willa Cather at the beginning of *My Antonia;* "to be dissolved into something complete and great."

Now a great university is many things — many very different and differing things — to many people. It is first of all the fountain of youth, and you will find George Saintsbury defending the largesse of privilege: "But exclude not from the beneficent splash and spray of the fountain those who are not prepared to drink very deep, and let them play pleasantly by its waters." Yet the fountain is too slender an image. My great university is the haven of scholars and teachers, the laboratory of scientists and technicians, the church of the theologian, the crow's nest of the visionary, the courtroom of the law, the forum of the public servant. It is gallery, concert hall, and stage; the out-patient ward for the medical student, counting-house of the businessman, classroom of the nation, lecture platform for the visitor, library to the world; and (on the recent word of a Harvard alumnus) "one of the great achievements of American democracy."

It is typical that Harvard offers a way into almost anything, and an exit for those intellectually prepared to endure a winter of reason against a summer of pragmatic doubt. James Stephens used to say that you don't learn the French language, you take it in through the pores. Harvard comes in through the pores. Her language is not always clear: it is not meant to be. It is sometimes like a page out of Whitehead or George Birkhoff; it may be the language of the calculus as George Washington Pierce used it to fill the blackboard on three sides of a room too large for six small amateurs in physics. It may be the language of overtone or implication, as once with Irving Babbitt; or a flawless, magnificent index of pursuit, as in the lectures of Lowes in a bygone English 72. It may be the urbanity of Fritz Robinson, whose Celtic and Chaucerian scholarship companion his bright speech.

Living on the periphery of a university one does not penetrate the classroom walls. But the intramural essence is there nonetheless; and ideas and argument seem to drift like smoke, much as the historian's observation of the Ogillallah village would suggest. Men of unusual ability electrify the air. To dwell in a community which holds or has held a Zechariah Chafee, a Nock, a Finley, a MacLeish, a Samuel Eliot Morison, a Harlow Shapley, a Raphael Demos, a Doc Davison or a G. Wallace Woodworth — to equal the Muses in number — and not to have discovered some new conception of individual liberty, classic wit, Greek thought, poetry as a weapon, history as delight, a populous infinity, table talk as inspiration, and choral music as a life-long joy, is almost an impossibility.

The past, as one winnows it, is spare and tidy. Pleasant images flit through the mind: E. K. Rand, beloved toastmaster-general — *Gratulor quod eum, quem necesse erat diligere.* Or Al Smith, one scalding Commencement day, cigar in his mouth, sweat on the brow, a pen in his hand, autographing the starched flare cuffs of the waitresses at the dignitaries' tent while Ambassadors Sir Ronald Lindsay and Paul Claudel watched with undisguised astonishment. Or Copey, seated on the steps of Hollis one June evening, the stain of misery on his face as a student asked him if he didn't consider Donald Ogden Stewart — whose writing the Sage admired and had often read aloud — a greater man than Dickens. Or the late Julian Coolidge, first Master of Lowell House, breezing into Billings & Stover on a winter evening in a red-lined opera cape and saying in all honesty to a strange young alumnus who had greeted him by name: "How did you know who I am?"

I return to the clearing in the wilderness. "Every thing looks permanent until its secret is known," said Emerson. One stammers in the light of revelation, for surely in this single sentence Harvard's premier aphorist has resolved the gist of what I have been trying to explain. His University endures and lays hold upon us because its secret defies the intellect. We examine it, we pry into it — but only to reassure ourselves that the whole of what it concerns is greater than the sum of its parts. It was Emerson again who spoke about the endless train of ghosts in the Yard at the time of the two hundred and fiftieth anniversary of the founding of the College. They returned from the Tercentenary in 1936. They are with us day and night to remind the careless that three centuries and one score over is a long time in American history. The Harvard ethos as a concentrate is powerful stuff. If the fallout from one atomic blast were as beneficent as that of my College we might do with but one word for the humanities and the sciences. I could wish that this were so.

David McCord received the A.B. degree from Harvard in 1921; A.M., 1922. As executive secretary of the Harvard Fund Council, he was the College tithing-man. He is also a poet and essayist. His books include "The Crows," "Far and Few," "Odds without Ends," "About Boston," and "What Cheer."

A Long-Term Bond with Harvard

Harvard for me in 1919 was a cornucopia containing prized packages of intellectual freedom, within broad but prescribed boundaries, and manifold opportunities to compete academically and in extracurricular activities. And it exemplified Christianity and humanism within the scope of varying backgrounds and relationships, with a principal ingredient, tolerance.

Armed with a Roxbury Latin School training in the basics but with complete naïveté about the bigger world, I appeared on my first day before my advisor, the famed English professor, Dr. [Charles] Copeland. As I emerged from the Harvard Square kiosk, a rain cloud burst; in an attempt to protect my attire I purchased my first umbrella. Unthinkingly, I left it against the chair in Dr. Copeland's entry room where it soon stood in the center of a large pool of water on his newly waxed floor. Dr. Copeland, after giving me some laissez-faire advice, politely showed me to the door. On seeing the puddle, he bellowed, "Who is the ill-bred pup who committed this nuisance?" I, of course, knew. Dr. Copeland, sensing my consternation, turned to a young man standing near and then to me and said, "Let me introduce my protégé, Tubby Clark!" Tubby Clark was a Phi Beta Kappa, an All-American football player, and the campus hero. Thereafter, whenever I saw Clark in the Yard his always cheerful words, "How are you doing, Al?" made me feel I belonged to Harvard.

Harvard exemplified tolerance for me. Dean [Chester] Greenough, an archetypical Puritan, taught a course in American Literature. When, a third of the way through his lectures, he dismissed Edgar Allen Poe with the pejorative words, "We now come to Edgar

Allen Poe. No one who led such a dissolute life could write great literature. We pass on to John Greenleaf Whittier," I resolved to put Greenough's biases to the test and I labored, in Poe's words, "long, singing a song . . . ", in a semi-major classic, to disprove Greenough's provocative assertion. The "A" he gave me proved to me that at Harvard one was not penalized for having an unfashionable opinion.

As I stated, Harvard to my mind connoted intellectual freedom. Any student reasonably well prepared could succeed in any course he selected. Though my major was economics, I was permitted to take a wide-ranging selection of courses, including one in music, another in the history of art, and four in ROTC — the latter because I was convinced that sooner rather than later there would be a second World War. Looking back, it seems to me Harvard has many of the attributes of a long-term bond. From his investment the student immediately received interest payments, and at maturity he received full benefits.

Harvard fostered competitiveness because no matter how good one was in any sport — except for a number-one man like Clark — someone was always better. How I longed to be a champion runner! I strove mightily to breast the tape but to no avail. There was always someone who beat me, and in my senior year I was humiliated to trail many a sophomore at the finish line.

Instruction often went beyond the classroom. Our Math professor told us that if we stayed after the bell he would attempt to tell us how to succeed in gambling: "You must not only contrast the odds of winning with those of losing, but also you must compare your potential gains with your potential losses. Try to be rational — if a coin comes up heads 16 times, don't bet the next time on tails—there must be something wrong with the coin. And, whether you like it or not, you will have to take many a gamble before your sun sets."

The next year Allen Young, at the time the leading authority on money and banking, told us, "I hope you lose the money on your speculations in German marks. In a year, the mark will be worthless. It will be a cheap price for you to learn about the consequences of inflation. Keynes may be right about the short-run benefits of government spending in a depression period, but he doesn't realize that few politicians will vote for deflation in a boom period."

Harvard today gives me a satisfying nostalgia. And why not? For better or worse, it has given me roots, the nourishing of which has given me euphoria. And it is a thrill to belong to a successfully evolving institution.

In 1919 wisdom was pervasive, much of it practical. All one had to do was to tune in on the academic channel to which one was attracted. Beyond in the real world, was life with all of its opportunities and challenges.

Albert Gordon '23 is Chairman of Kidder Peabody, Co-chairman of the Harvard Campaign, friend of Harvard athletics, inveterate jogger, and senior runner as well as a Trollope enthusiast.

JOHN L. LOEB

Enough Learning for a Lifetime

To me, Harvard has always been a special place, but the discovery of just how special has been more than 60 years in the making.

I came to Harvard in 1921, a transfer student from Dartmouth, bringing with me a healthy bump of intellectual curiosity, a desire to make lasting friends, and an ardent interest in sports, although my name will never be found in any hall of fame. In fact, my undergraduate years were not especially noteworthy. I can recall only one incident in my athletic "career" that attracted much attention. Finding that I was barred as a transferee for one year from intercollegiate athletics, I decided to take up rowing. One day, while still a neophyte, I resolved to test my progress with a trial run in a single scull. Despite warnings from Coach Haines and others that it was too windy, I persisted. Fifty feet from the boathouse, I capsized and found myself thrashing around in the water, to the cheers and jeers of the onlookers. That was not my day, but ultimately I had the satisfaction of earning a place in my class boat.

Because I missed my first year in the Freshman dormitories and was too comfortable in a suite in Randolph Hall to move to the Yard in my senior year, I had little direct contact with my classmates. Thus, my friends tended to come from other classes and the graduate schools. They were few but cherished. Many a Saturday night we met for dinner at Ye Olde Cockhorse Inn and dedicated ourselves to becoming slightly drunk — fun, but *de rigueur* for those prohibition times.

The passing years have given me an ever-growing appreciation of the enduring values of my Harvard education. Certainly my critical judgments of literature were sharpened by inspired teachers:

Bliss Perry, Kittredge, the scholarly Lowes, and Kirsop Lake, whose title, the Winn Professor of Ecclesiastical History, somehow seemed too pompous for such an emotionally involved yet simple and kindly man. And I am sure it was Professor Edgell's course in fine arts that laid the foundation for my lifelong interest in art collecting.

Gus(tafus) Maynadier was not only a distinguished philologist, but also a sensitive and observant friend. One afternoon, I was having tea with him at his home. Because I was anxious to keep a low profile, I was wearing my usual wrinkled slacks and a frayed sports jacket. Out of a blue sky, he gave me a quizzical look and said, "One of the things I have always liked about you is your prosperous look."

When I graduated in 1924, I was grateful for an education second to none. But it was years later that Harvard was to become a much greater factor in my life. Through service on several Visiting Committees, deep involvement with A Program for Harvard College, and, most of all, six rewarding years from 1962 through 1968 as an Overseer, I came to understand a strange truth. The more I have served Harvard and the more I have given to Harvard, the more indebted to Harvard I have become. The reasons for this anomaly are not hard to find.

During the years since my graduation, I have been called on to work with an awesome array of brilliant men and women, drawn from the University's faculties and alumni leaders from around the world: physicians whose imaginative research is opening doorways to healthier lives for all of us; city planners and designers whose visions for tomorrow give promise of enriching our daily lives by improving the environment in which we live. Scientists, authors, artists, administrators, lawyers, business leaders, and more — surely their collective wisdom is a national treasure beyond compare. Involvement with such as these has been a rare and challenging experience for which I am humbly grateful.

Yes, Harvard is a very special place. It is different from and superior to other institutions of learning in the quality of its leadership, and the excellence and diversity of its faculty and student body.

Mr. Lowell, who was president of Harvard during my stay at Cambridge, was wont to say, "The mark of an educated man is the ability to make a reasoned guess on the basis of insufficient information." On the basis of his definition, I suppose I am an educated man, having made enough good guesses from time to time to support Harvard and other worthy institutions.

Many men of Harvard have become great leaders in their own right, in many different fields; many of us have not. But generations of caring alumni have proved that each of us can, in his own way and to the best of his ability, leave his footprints on the sands of time by supporting Harvard. In this way we can be sure that in the years to come Harvard will continue to turn out great men and women, not only to the advantage of Harvard, and our country, but to the world as well.

John Langeloth Loeb '24, banker, broker, philanthropist, a former member of the Board of Overseers, former Chairman, Finance Committee, Loeb, Rhoades, Hornblower and Co., received an honorary LL.D. from Harvard in 1971.

37 Years a Student

I have been a student at Harvard for thirty-seven years. Those of my fellow students with whom I am most closely associated call me professor, treat me with respect and affection, and seem to think I know more than they do. When they leave Harvard, they remain in my vast and growing family, and I have occasional telephone calls, "This is Jim. Remember me? Class of '32." They give me news of their successes and their frustrations, and they send me compositions.

Every so often I am asked if it is good for a composer to teach in a university like Harvard, and if Harvard is a good place for a student with the urge to write music. An answer to that question should begin by saying that composers are nonconformist individuals and that what is good for one is not of necessity good for all. The composer has a primary and essential duty to preserve and cultivate his own individuality. It is his lifelong preoccupation to discover just what he must express in music and how best to express it. These goals are not to be lost sight of in choosing a means of livelihood. And a living must be gained outside the career of composing, for we must realize that in today's world new music, except in a few special fields, is not a commodity.

In more and more colleges, and particularly at Harvard, the composer now finds he is valued as a creative artist. The fact that he is a practicing composer possessing a certain demonstrated mastery of his art is taken to mean that what he may be able to impart in the way of knowledge and advice to students will be a worth-while contribution to their education. The atmosphere of a place where learning is going on is conducive and sympathetic to creative writing. Not the least of the advantages is that of being with young people of that particular age. Their keen curiosity and wealth of ideas annihilate complacency and compel one to see to the continuity of one's own education. Their lively interest in the creative work of the teacher-composer is extremely stimulating, to say nothing of the inestimable worth to him of their critical comments. In the two-way discussions on all sorts of questions I sense at times that the roles of teacher and student become interchanged.

Turning to the question from the standpoint of the budding student-composer, there appears to be no doubt that he profits greatly from the broadening intellectual environment that Harvard, as a liberal arts college, provides. He needs studies in the history and literature of music. Training in the technical branches of composition is necessarily incomplete (it will not be finished in a lifetime), but he will be in a position to receive orientation and knowledge, to guide him toward the achievement of self-education. His leanings to creative activity and independent thinking will be encouraged, and will find fertile ground for growing. And he, like the composer-teacher, will inevitably look back upon his association with fellow students in music as a richly rewarding and unforgettable cultural and human experience.

Walter H. Piston received the degree of A.B. from Harvard in 1924. A well known composer, he was appointed a Professor of Music at Harvard in 1944. He received the Pulitzer Prize in Music in 1948.

The Wit of President Lowell

My warmest memory of Harvard goes back to a September day in Cambridge in 1922 when our class of 1926 was gathered in the vast central hall of the Harvard Union for the official welcome from President Lowell.

"Gentlemen," he began (how he loved the word "gentleman" — and how he made us all want to be one). "Gentlemen, you have a vast horizon before you. After four years, and upon graduation, you will move out into the world as part of Harvard's great fellowship of educated men. There you will find fellow graduates who have won distinction in every walk of life. They are everywhere — in Rome, Toledo, Tokyo, Hong Kong, Kamchatka, Timbuktu . . ."

A dramatic pause. And then: "In fact, gentlemen," Lowell went on, "there is even a Harvard Club in the San Quentin prison in California and I am told that its membership is increasing rapidly."

Not much of a story. But in an odd way it sums up Harvard's strength — which comes from a strangely magic mixture of unity and diversity.

For me, the unity is personified by A. Lawrence Lowell himself. He was an example, if ever there was one, of the "relic and type of our ancestors' worth" — a living symbol of more than three centuries of Harvard heritage and tradition.

But from this rock-strong center, the Harvard universe stretches out, with infinite variety, infinite curiosity, infinite imagination, infinite transgression, and infinite tolerance to the four corners of the world — even including cells in the San Quentin prison and a tomb outside the Kremlin walls.

It was one of Lowell's proudest boasts that "there is a Harvard man on the wrong side of every question." God bless them all. But most of all, God bless him.

William I. Nichols '26 is former editor of This Week *magazine, former Freshman Dean and former Director of the Harvard University News Office.*

An Island of Light

I came to Harvard in the autumn of 1924, an unintimidated freshman in an expectant and receptive mood. My first impression, as I
suppose is true of most new students who come to Cambridge from
the Midwest, was a sense of the history around me illustrated by
Harvard's old buildings and other evidences of a notable past of
which I was only vaguely conscious through my reading. But my
second impression was of my classmates — or at least the first group
of them I met.

The first time I entered the dining hall of Gore, which was then
a freshman dormitory, I went to the nearest empty chair. As I sat
down, I said hello to my two or three nearest neighbors. They must
at least have looked in my direction; perhaps they may well have
grunted a response to my greeting, as a minimum concession to
etiquette. But my clear recollection is that with very little recognition of my presence they went right on talking animatedly among
themselves.

What talk it seemed to be! Shaw, Ibsen, Nietzsche. Back and
forth the conversation went, in the clever fragmented sentences of
quick repartee. Before dessert they had gone on to Katherine
Mansfield, and then in a postprandial few minutes they dealt, to
their satisfaction and mine, with Cabell and Mencken.

This was not the kind of talk which experience with contemporaries back home had led me to expect. I was at once amazed,
terrified, excited, and pleased. And so began my experience of
Harvard.

The names of the authors discussed so confidently at that meal
have remained in my memory, for though I may have heard of

them before coming to Harvard, I certainly had not read them, and later, as I discovered them for myself, their names were driven into my memory. Each time I met one, I recalled the sick feeling I had had that first night when I came to Harvard alone — my first trip east of Chicago — and was confronted with the incredible, if perhaps — may I add this now? — slightly pretentious erudition of a select new group of Harvard undergraduates clearly much better prepared for what lay ahead than I. But may I also say that the great respect I acquired for Harvard undergraduates at that time, though it may since have changed character, has never been diminished in even slight degree by prolonged association with them.

Dare I admit that now my most vivid recollection of my first year's study is a phrase from a freshman German examination? The teacher of this course was a lively young German graduate student, a superb teacher, whose name, unfortunately, has long since left me. For our final examination in sight reading he had written in German a short, whimsical account of an American movie. Perhaps he had the senior Douglas Fairbanks in mind. At any rate in the first few sentences the hero was shown performing a series of incredible physical exploits. Next we were shown the heroine in peril, drowning in a mountain lake. As I recall, the text then ran something like this: "But don't worry, it is now nearly eleven o'clock, and since this is a movie all must soon end happily." At once the hero appeared from nowhere, dove into the lake, thrashed about madly, if ostentatiously, and finally pulled the heroine safe to shore. Immediately the camera came close to reveal her in his arms, dry, beautiful, and perfectly groomed, and then, at the end, moved from the handsome, happy couple, to show a little dog who looked on (the typical movie fade-out of the period) *"und wedelt mit dem Schwanze."*

I imagine we were supposed to be learning which cases followed which prepositions, but this particular teacher, like so many teachers at Harvard, was teaching a great deal more than the immediate matter in hand. It was his guiding idea, I suppose, that to get on in the world we should learn to be critical; but it was also salutary for us that in his practice criticism was always characterized by good humor.

A year or two later I had found my way into courses of John Livingston Lowes and Irving Babbitt. From that time each day was filled with what were to me fresh ideas and excited inspiration to read and go on learning. Professor Lowes' course in sixteenth and seventeenth century lyric poetry was one of the first at Harvard which for me seemed completely to break through the limitations of the containing course. It was not so much an exercise in learning as an experience of life itself. There was much in the course of interest and delight, but what chiefly remains now is an image of Lowes reading — one might almost say barking — an endless flood of lyric poetry with such delight that one could not fail to feel its enchantment.

> It was a lover and his lass,
> With a hey, and a ho, and a hey nonino.

> Tell me where is Fancy bred,
> Or in the heart or in the head?

> If she think not well of me,
> What care I how fair she be?

And there is Babbitt, rolling a pencil between his hands, looking over the tops of his glasses, saying of Tennyson's *Locksley Hall*: "This scientific belief in the far-off divine event is nothing other than a form of nostalgia, an offshoot of the Romantic imagination, illegitimately associated with the religious virtue Peace." It was heady stuff for a young student finding his way into the world of ideas. This and much more of the kind in endless profusion. Whatever one thought of Babbitt's point of view, there was never any mistaking that he had one, nor any reason to doubt that he was every day dealing with matters of immense and urgent importance. From him one learned more than ever that life and learning are not to be separated — that what one thinks matters! He was a superlative pedagogue whose classes were full of import, broadly conceived as few would now dare — and never dull.

The intimate experiences of Harvard are, of course, as individual and as numerous as the students who come here. Today it may be that I am more aware of and impressed by the variety and range of intellectual interest represented in the great faculty of the whole University, and by the faculty's importance both for enriching the known and for keeping alive the possibility for learning, than I am perhaps by students. But fortunately there is no need to set these two groups against each other. They both belong; together they make Harvard.

In the complex and confused world in which we all find ourselves it is possible to think of Harvard as a kind of island of light in a very widespread darkness, and I must confess I sometimes do just this. But I also know that the figure is not really an apt one, for Harvard has never been an island severed from the broad concerns of men and is certainly not one now. Instead, it is rather intimately involved in the complex culture to which it belongs. Its distinction is that in it intellectual activity has an opportunity to come into sharper focus, and so becomes richer, more vivid, more convincing, and more captivating than in society at large.

As the freshman comes into this place he cannot fail to be impressed by the extraordinary liveliness, concentration and devotion with which learning long has been and is now pursued — nor can a President!

Nathan M. Pusey received the degree of A.B. from Harvard in 1928; A.M., 1932; Ph.D., 1937. He served as President of Harvard University from 1953 to 1971.

Sophomoric Aplomb

As a sophomore, in my choice of courses I tried to ride off in all directions at once. In cantering along the highways and byways of the College's offerings, I chanced upon George Foote Moore's course on the History of Religions. I wandered in for a tentative nibble, became hungry, and remained.

Under the impression that Moore was my personal discovery, I made inquiries about him. In due course, it was borne in upon me that he was a man of prodigious learning, widely regarded as perhaps the University's first scholar. He bore the weight of his learning lightly. To the callow sophomore before him, the flow of his knowledge seemed as natural and friendly as the flow of the Mississippi to a youngster at play along its banks.

This, I decided, was the career for me. I would scintillate as a scholar in the History of Religions. So momentous a decision, it seemed clear to me, must be communicated without delay to Professor Moore. On a spring evening, after dinner, I set off for his house. I climbed the steps of the old porch, untroubled by the thought that I had neither written nor phoned for an appointment. My great decision had filled my mind, excluding the possibility of thought about the familiar amenities. It had also buried the obvious fact that, as an obscure student in a lecture course, neither my name nor my face would mean anything to Moore.

I rang the bell, and waited. When Moore came to the door, peering through the gloom, his expression would have made it clear to a perceptive eye that he had anticipated no visitors for the evening. Yet, when his eye made out the unexpected and unfamiliar figure on his doorstep, he smiled warmly, and greeted me with a "Won't you come in?"

He received my great announcement with grave and interested courtesy. We talked about it at length and in many aspects, through a long and wonderful evening. Through gentle questions which emerged unobtrusively in the course of our talk, he gradually made me dimly aware of some of the implications of the undertaking. Through what channel did I plan to enter the field of study? Philology, like his colleague Dr. Lanman? Philosophy? Oriental Studies? Anthropology?

So the ancient lessons were brought home to me as a fresh and personal insight of my own. It was entirely right and natural to want to fly, but first one had to have ground school training and a mastery of technique. By all means, choose exploration and pioneering and high adventure, but first master your maps, your means of transport, your weapons and instruments. In this, George Foote Moore reflected a primary element in the essence of Harvard College: to welcome and nourish aspiration, however awkward and unexpected its initial appearance, and to insist that the right to aspiration must be earned through discipline and its pursuit supported by proficiency.

Milton Katz received the degree of A.B. from Harvard in 1927; LL.B., 1931. He served as chief of U.S. Delegation Economic Commission for Europe in 1950–51. He is Henry L. Stimson Professor of Law and Director of International Legal Studies at Harvard.

JOHN K. FAIRBANK

From Peking Man
To Mao Tse-Tung

Compared with today, being a Harvard undergraduate in the 1920s
was a comparatively grim and narrow experience. In 1927 I roomed
in Randolph Hall, five flights up, looking down on the Lampoon
building. Dark panelling made our rooms rather dingy but at least
the bedmaker tidied them up every day except Sunday. In any case,
we had no time for aesthetic concerns. Milk was delivered to our
door (there were still services in those days) and we bought Shredded Wheat by the case, 24 boxes at a time. Lunch and dinner we
wolfed down after lining up at the Georgian Cafeteria on Dunster
Street. For variety we sometimes went to the Georgian on the
Square, where Brigham's now is, and ordered our chicken a la king
at the rear counter. (We never could decide how much of the
chicken was really veal).

My roommate and I knew classmates from Exeter, who formed
the largest single component among Harvard undergraduates, and
we met others in classes in the Yard. But both of us were preoccupied
mastering our subjects and had little time for social activities. After
the first hour exams, the climate got darker and colder, punctuated
by the waxing and waning of pale sunlight and the alternation of
snowfalls and slush. Soon we were in our winter underwear and
galoshes, sloshing along the hand-shoveled board walks through
the Yard and crossing Mass. Ave. on the cobblestones that en-
shrined the streetcar tracks. It was a busy, molelike winter on the
books, exciting because we were acquiring an education in large

and fundamental subjects. We led a life of scholarly concentration, calling it Harvard individualism.

In 1929 President Lowell announced the House Plan. We heard that a Yale millionaire, Mr. Harkness, had found New Haven a bit uncertain about the idea of building Oxford-Cambridge-type residential colleges to take the place of dormitories. When Mr. Harkness brought his idea to Cambridge, President Lowell said to him, "Yes, I've been thinking about that and here are the architectural plans we have prepared."

In the Senior Council, a group of about 10, we were quite suspicious about Mr. Lowell's House Plan. What would it do to the Harvard individualism of which we felt ourselves to be the custodians? Having known nothing better and yet risen to our temporary eminence on this powerless advisory body, we found ourselves extraordinarily conservative about the system that had produced us. Mr. Lowell was about to create a new Harvard for a new age that would integrate scholarship with culture and help civilize the young men and even young women of America's future. But having eaten individualistically for so long in those Georgian cafeterias, I remember questioning Mr. Lowell, at a Senior Council meeting we had with him in the Faculty Room. I asked him whether his House Plan with its collective amenities bringing students together as in prep schools might not undermine the stalwart virtues of Harvard individualism. Mr. Lowell gave me a rather short answer. I got the idea that he had been thinking about the matter for more years than I had been around.

As an undergraduate I was at first below the level of contact with great teachers. I probably got the most from the course in which I had to do the most work. *History 1* gave me my picture of what had happened since 410 A.D. The course was a monster headed by Roger Bigelow Merriman, a stentorian lecturer who could be heard even in the anti-acoustics of the New Lecture Hall. (It is now named

for President Lowell, who had anonymously given it to Harvard.)
He concluded his last lecture by letting a piece of chalk on a string
swing back and forth in front of the blackboard like a pendulum.
"Action and reaction," he bellowed. We got the message of history
— left and right, revolution and reaction, renaissance and reformation, rise and fall. Everybody clapped.

This was only *History 1*'s surface appearance. There was also a
weekly quiz, as part of a section meeting, plus a map to hand in
and a reading report, all concatenated by a devoted schoolmaster,
Paul P. Cram, who had a staff of a dozen instructors equipped with
lists of required readings and possible term paper topics. Having
the story of the rise of Europe to convey — all the countries with
their cities, rulers, movements, and institutions — *History 1* could
hardly stop short of exhausting the subject, the students and the
instructors. We had a bear by the tail. The course was practically
as big as all the rest of the History Department; and 10 years later,
shortly after I came back to Harvard as a young instructor, it had
to be dismantled.

The other survey course from which I learned the most was
William L. Langer's *History 2, Modern Europe,* a skillful, wide-ranging,
and dramatic combination of political, economic, social and dip-
lomatic history. Survey courses that gave us all the world, plus or
minus a few areas, were part of the heroic if simple-minded charm
of the 1920s. After 1946 the all-encompassing spirit of *History 1*
and *History 2* moved me and Edwin O. Reischauer to produce
another protean survey, *The History of East Asian Civilization.* Turning
a survey spotlight on one-third of humankind in East Asia was
another opportunity to fill a vacuum. Between Peking Man and
Mao Tse-tung, we galloped through the ages, setting up milestones
along the way. In China, students learned to distinguish Wang
Mang, Wang An-shih, Wang Yang-ming and Wang-Ching-wei,
who were men, from *wang tao,* the way of the ruler. This prepared
the American citizen, we hoped, to appreciate China's and Japan's

differentness and complexity. Even (or especially) after our wars in Korea and Vietnam, such an appreciation is still needed.

John King Fairbank '29 is Henry Higginson Professor of History, Emeritus, and a leading sinologist.

A Loyalty that Grows and Grows

The impact of Harvard on my life has been a continuing one. At a very early age, wonder grew into curiosity as I listened to my father whose life was closely tied to the University as Treasurer. At first, there were stories of the doings and sayings of Presidents Eliot and Lowell, with whom my father had worked intimately for many years. Then came football games with enough hoopla to capture the fancy of most growing boys; but curiously, I became even more intrigued by the conversations to which I listened attentively on the back piazza of the Glades, that unique and curious institution where we spent out summers. Of an evening, the gathering might include Robert Homans, Nelson Perkins, and Dr. Roger Lee, together with my father. All were members of the Corporation, so that the talk inevitably turned to Harvard. The most common subject revolved around the relative importance of the college and the graduate schools. Always, the debate was earnest, and the outcome inconclusive!

Of course the undergraduate years, when all the talk became reality, provided the primary experience and the centerpiece of my memories. If I have developed an eye for beauty in its various forms, I owe this to Professors Post, Edgell, and Sachs of the Fine Arts department. Meanwhile, the stimulus of my father and his friends receded, for he moved to Washington during my years in college. I do, however, remember well that when he did come back to Boston, there were most intriguing discussions with my Uncle, Bob Homans, of the prolonged search process which resulted in the appointment of James B. Conant to succeed Lawrence Lowell as president. To me as a junior, President Lowell was an awe-inspiring figure. One can imagine how startled I was one day when on entering my room in Lowell House I found the President, accompanied by his spaniel and the British Ambassador, who was a friend of my father's. Mr. Lowell was poking at my possessions with his stick, while they awaited my return. To this day, I have no explanation for his odd behavior.

Then came the Business School, an environment with quite a different character. Although my years there added essential knowledge and excellent preparation for a career in business, they could never to the same extent evoke such affectionate memories as the College.

In 1936, the Tercentenary celebrations served to impress me strongly with Harvard's place among the great universities of the world. We had the privilege of entertaining distinguished visitors, and thus taking part in numerous interesting events, but the high point was Tercentenary Day when my cousin George Homans and I acted as Marshals, representing the Class of '32. The presence of President Roosevelt, the voice from across the sea of Prime Minister Stanley Baldwin bringing, as Chancellor, the greetings of Cambridge University, and the sharing of an umbrella in the drenching rain with Lucius Littauer are vivid memories. Service on several visiting committees followed, providing new insights into the College; then came the most rewarding experience of all. For six years as an Overseer, the problems and progress of the University were laid before us. As we struggled to give useful advice and to arrive at wise judgments, our commitment to the University deepened. Now as we get rebriefed, better to serve The Harvard Campaign, we are once more enormously impressed by the leadership of the University in creating the Core Curriculum and the astonishing development of the School of Government.

Thus Harvard, always intriguing and ever changing, has been

the subject of continuing interest and growing attachment over at least 60 years of my life, rather than just for four. How can one resist this ongoing exposure to excellence?

Charles F. Adams '32 is a consultant and the Chairman of the Finance Committee for the Raytheon Company, Lexington, Massachusetts, where he was Chairman of the Board and Chief Executive Officer for 27 years. A former Overseer and member of numerous Visiting Committees, he celebrated his 50th reunion in 1982.

How to Escape Academe

On a recent evening at a lively dinner at Dunster House, I was asked by the hospitable master, Professor Raoul Bott, if, in introducing his several guests, he could ask me one question. A little nervously I said, "Of course." The question was: "How did you escape academe?"

I had no difficulty in supplying the answer: that, as a senior, I couldn't wait to get out. I was 21 and had been at school since the age of five. I had had enough of that occupation, and did not want to prolong it one more day. Nor did I want to take another exam as long as I lived.

Besides, in that year of 1933, the world was seething with events — Roosevelt had just been inaugurated, bringing to Washington the new Deal; Hitler had come to power in Germany, bringing ominous threats for the uncertain democratic nations, and with all this happening outside, I wanted to be in it, in some way, not enclosed within these protective walls.

Miss Comstock, then President of Radcliffe, opened the pathway for my emergence when, as a Board Member of the Institute of Pacific Relations, she gave them names of possible student apprentices in international relations, including mine. I applied and was duly accepted as a volunteer. Thus, the moment the doors of Briggs Hall and Agassiz closed behind me I was ready to set my feet on the road to the "real world." In addition, my grandfather had just been appointed a delegate to the World Economic Conference in London, and had invited me to come along, supplying an extra push in a direction away from the Harvard Yard. Indeed, I did not even wait for my own graduation.

To tell the truth, I had never for an instant even contemplated graduate school. For some reason I did not think of myself as a scholar, much less a teacher, which, I gathered, was what you went to graduate school to become. To be a teacher was not for me. I wanted to be, in some vague way, a writer; I did not know just how or in what form, but I was sure the form would not develop from more academic study.

One incident that confirmed my turning aside was the comment on a history paper I had handed in for Professor E. A. Whitney's *History II (History of England During the Tudor and Stuart Periods)*. The paper contrasted Thomas More and Machiavelli, as two voices of the Renaissance. I poured into it all my enthusiasm for research, and my rather unpolished literary talents, and felt I had delivered myself of a shining product. It was returned with a stingy mark of A-, followed by the comment, scrawled in large handwriting on my title page. "You spelled Philip with two l's;" not a word about the content or composition or ideas, if any.

It was a slap with impact that can be remembered now after half a century has passed and it meant to me then a disregard for substance coupled with a pedantic concern for mode that I believed represented the academic attitude. It did not occur to me that it more probably represented a tired mind, perhaps of an overworked section man threshing its way through a bundle of undergraduate papers, or that the comment was intended quite legitimately to stress the importance of accuracy. I simply took it as a narrowness of mind that repelled me and certainly did not invite or encourage any desire for academic pursuits. In addition, it created a life long aversion to Philip II of Spain. It is an eerie thought that some mute, inglorious section man unthinkingly helped to shape my career.

This is not to say that I did not enjoy the work at college: in fact, I did and was very stimulated by the courses in History and Lit. which was my major. And I shall always be grateful for the magic casements my professors opened to me and the wide horizons they brought into view — and, especially, for the treasury of sources that were made available to an inquiring student in the stacks at Widener. I think that of all my time at Radcliffe, I was happiest in the stacks, next to the experience of participating in the 'B' Minor Mass under Woody (Wallace Woodworth, Director, Radcliffe Choral), Doc Davidson (Conductor of the Harvard Glee Club), and Kousevitsky (Conductor of Chorus of the Boston Symphony). I say "participating" rather than singing since I could not sing on pitch, and was miserably rejected from Choral the first time I tried out, but happily I had a beau (as a boyfriend was called in those days), who was manager of the Harvard Glee Club, and used his pull to get me into the Chorus for the Mass.

To emerge from Sever into a sharp winter's night and walk home across the yard with "om-ni-po-TEN-tem," and the quick triumphant notes of *"Et resurrexit"* sounding inside one's head was living at a peak of verve and beauty, like coming out the first person in the morning on a ski slope of untrodden snow freshly fallen the night before. I think that the 'B' Minor Mass and Widener were the two richest parts of my life at Radcliffe.

Barbara Q. Tuchman '33, is a writer, historian, and two-time Pulitzer Prize-winner, whose latest book, The March of Folly (Knopf) was a bestseller.

THE CONANT YEARS

1933 – 1953

The Day It Rained

We had talked about the day for more than a year. Indeed, Tom Slocum declared that if he heard one more speech about plans for the Tercentenary Celebration, he would believe that he had already been there. As to the exact date, there had been, at first, some question. The founding of a college is not like the birth of a baby; it is not an event which can be said to have occurred on a certain day. Historians can usually find good reasons why any one of a number of dates might be designated as "the day" when the "the founding" took place. The vote of the General Court which established Harvard College was passed on November 7, 1636. But November, we argued, is clearly not a good month for a celebration. College would be in session, football interest would be nearing its peak, the weather uncertain. Unless one were satisfied with a simple indoor ceremony attended by a relatively small number, another month had better be found.

Fortunately, some one remembered that the General Court which established the college later to be called Harvard, first convened on September 18, 1636 (old style or new style, I cannot recall). So, September 18, 1936 would be "the day." After this date had been "cleared" with Sam Morison, the official historian, everyone was happy. The big affair would be held in the College Yard without interfering with college business and the weather promised to be good. Of course, a day in October would be more certain. Mr. Lowell, it was said, had picked a day in that month for his inauguration after examining the weather records for fifty years or so. And the weather had been perfect. But the same records also provided a favorable prognosis for September. Indeed, so favorable were the predictions, that as late as mid-July no plans had been made for the eventuality of wet weather. But an alternative was eventually constructed; though I remember Jerome Greene's saying something to the effect that it could hardly be called an alternative, since the audience would be cut from 10,000 to about 1,000, the capacity of Sanders Theatre.

We considered the possibility of a tent, — this was the period of the tented Commencements behind Sever. But a tent large enough to shelter the audience we envisioned would not only look like, but probably be, a circus tent. So we developed plans for seating 10,000 people between Widener and the Church and trusted that the weather would be good. It was, on September 17, the day of the meeting of the Associated Harvard Clubs, — a meeting which provided the first test of our plans. After that day was done, we went to bed full of confidence for the morrow. Indeed, even a last-minute check before breakfast on the 18th, — *the* day, — by Jerome Greene, indicated no precipitation unless a little hurricane which was out at sea should suddenly change its course. When I received this message, I waved aside the remote contingency of a hurricane's changing its course so as to interfere with our celebration. (This was before New England became hurricane conscious.) We breakfasted without worry and, leaving my guests to robe, I walked to the Massachusetts Avenue entrance of Widener, hardly noticing the overcast sky.

Confusion before an academic procession starts is traditional. Scholars put on their robes and wander about greeting friends and disobeying instructions. I was in the middle of the confusions in the lower hall of Widener, welcoming guests, when suddenly I looked at the gown on the person whose hand I was shaking. There seemed to be water on it! Involuntarily I reached forward, swept my fingers over the front of the gown and drew back my hand in horror. "Your gown is wet," I exclaimed. "Yes," the guest replied, "it's raining, didn't you know it?"

The Day It Rained

We went through with the morning exercises according to schedule. It drizzled and the tall silk hats and the gowns got wetter and wetter. The audience did not flinch, however, though some put up umbrellas. Three-quarters of the way through the program, there was a brief let-up and then, as the final hymn was sung, the skies opened and it poured. Robert Blake won immortal fame by miraculously providing whiskey for the dripping academic dignitaries when the procession returned to the library. The afternoon alumni meeting was held in Sanders Theatre. What was said by Presidents Roosevelt, Lowell and Angell will be remembered by the few who were lucky enough to squeeze in. The President of Yale's remark about his colleague's way of "soaking the rich" has become part of Harvard's folklore. People even spoke kindly of the morning exercises. Indeed, there were many who declared that the entire day had been an historic occasion. But as I look back upon it, of only one thing I am absolutely sure: it really rained.

James B. Conant received the A.B. degree from Harvard in 1913; Ph.D. in chemistry, 1916. He served as Harvard's President from 1933 to 1953. After serving as U.S. Ambassador to Germany, he conducted important research on American high schools.

HELEN GILBERT

The Harvard World
of a Bostonian

It was a bright, clear June day in 1970, the day of Harvard's Commencement. Radcliffe students had celebrated their Commencement in the morning in the Radcliffe Yard, and I had partaken of the usual Presidential lunch at 76 Brattle Street; but my mind was on the Alumni exercises in the Harvard Yard. I was up for election as an Overseer. I had been told my chances were slim, as I "had no friends west of Milton," and the Radcliffe franchise was not then in effect. Bob Gardiner, Radcliffe's Treasurer and a devoted Harvard alumnus, urged me on to the Harvard festivities. As I remember it, we ran most of the way, breathlessly rounding University Hall just in time to hear the names of the newly elected Overseers called out. The wait seemed interminable. Mine was the last name called.

That evening I dined with my cousin Charles Adams. I asked if his father and my father, former Treasurer and Fellow respectively, wouldn't have been pleased at my election to the Board of Overseers. Chas, replied, "Can't you hear my father say, 'My dear girl, that is no place for a woman.'"

I grew up in Boston's Back Bay, first on Marlboro Street, later on Beacon Hill. In those days of the '20s and early '30s, we weren't exactly one big, happy family, but my family knew many who lived there and, as children, we romped over the whole area. It was homogeneous, made up mostly of professional men and their families. Most were educated at New England preparatory schools for their entrance to Harvard, which was the center of their interest, shared only with their medical or legal careers. Such men as Drs. Cheever, Zinsser, and Cushing; Charles P. Curtis, a Fellow of Harvard; C. F. Adams, Harvard's Treasurer, and the great oarsman, Hugh Bancroft. Serving Harvard was a great honor, recognized as such throughout the Boston community.

While I was still a young girl, my father Robert Homans served briefly on the Corporation as a Fellow and participated in the election of James Bryant Conant as Harvard's President. My father adored Harvard, and was very proud of his Class of '94. He also served at that time as Grand Marshal of the Porcellian Club, and I remember vividly dinners at 289 Marlboro Street when those members were entertained.

The Homans family had long been associated with Harvard, principally as distinguished surgeons at the Harvard teaching hospitals. In my youth, Uncle Dr. John Homans regaled his nieces and nephews with hilarious tales of his teaching methods and with the students' reactions to them. On my mother's side, the Adamses had not only been part of the American scene; they, too, had been heavily involved with Harvard, almost since Harvard's founding.

The Harvard orbit surrounding my family, relatives, and family friends became somewhat overwhelming. As I passed through Miss Winsor's School and boarding school in Connecticut, there seemed to be such a straight and narrow path ahead — to marry a Harvard man and live happily ever after in Boston. I began to feel a bit rebellious.

Wanting to live at home after three years in the boarding school atmosphere, I took my college boards and applied to Radcliffe — I think all it took at that time was a telephone call and a $400 deposit. I was accepted, and began my own heady experience with the Harvard faculty. Perhaps because my older brother George was in sociology, and quoting Pareto, and my sister at Radcliffe, majoring in fine arts, I dived into biology. Professor Carroll Williams gave me my first A, and thus I was jet-propelled into a medical career. I could follow my Homans grandparent and uncle, and I was urged on by Dr. Zinsser, who lived near us. Professor Feiser, lecturer in Organic Chemistry, was truly inspirational and one of Harvard's greats. Harvard had begun to lure me back to its fold.

I didn't marry a Harvard man. At least I broke that tradition. He was a graduate of the University of Virginia — *the* University, but he was also a graduate of *the* Law School, and was practicing law at Ropes and Gray — that most Harvard of all the Boston law firms.

It was in the mid-'50s that President [Wilbur K.] Jordan asked me to become a trustee of Radcliffe, beginning for me an association of almost 25 years. The Radcliffe by-laws state that three Harvard professors shall serve on the Radcliffe Board for a term of three years. Thus it was that I came to know Arthur Schlesigner, Sr., Bart Bok, Reuben Brower, Bobby Wolf, Zeph Stewart, Emily Vermeule and so many more. They kept the Radcliffe-Harvard connection on a solid course and added greatly to my knowledge of the Harvard faculty and the institution itself.

Oh my! There were some snags to my Harvard relationship. Early in 1965, when President [Mary] Bunting went to Washington, I was acting President of Radcliffe; innocently I gave permission for some Radcliffe cheerleaders to appear at a New England Patriots football game. A very irate Harvard Dean called me just prior to the game. "Get your girls off John Harvard," he commanded peremptorily. The Patriot's public relations man had them draped over the statue in front of University Hall, dressed in blue sweaters emblazoned with a large, white P.

There were also some messy moments during the merger/non-merger negotiations with Dean [John] Dunlop over Radcliffe's drain of the faculty budget — but even money matters didn't dampen my ever increasing respect for Harvard.

Now, after six years as an Overseer, I can look back and realize that I have come full circle, and that most of my life has been connected with Harvard. Thus, to the "My dear girl, that is no place for a woman," I would reply, "It has been a most rewarding and important place for *this* woman."

Helen Homans Gilbert '36 (Mrs. Carl J.) served on the Radcliffe Board of Trustees from 1950 to 1972 and was chairman from 1955 to 1972. She was the first woman to serve on Harvard's Board of Overseers, from 1970 to 1976. In 1964–65 she served as Acting President of Radcliffe College.

JOHN PAPPENHEIMER

Notes and Footnotes

F.D.R. had been in office for eight months and 3.2% beer was on its way to the Square. Upperclassmen were testing out the new House plan along the river, leaving the Yard to President Lowell, his blind cocker spaniel, and the Tercentenary Class of 1936. We, the freshmen, were observers of the Great Depression but most of us were not a part of it. Harvard had yet to reach out for the best and brightest from across the land and we took for granted a Certificate of Admission from Henry Pennypacker and full financial support from our parents. To paraphrase T. S. Eliot:

> "We came this way, taking the route we were most likely to take
> From the place we would most likely come from. . . .
> Either we had no purpose or the purpose was beyond the end we had
> figured and was altered in fulfillment."

Truth to tell, I came because my father, brother, and sister had led the way and none of us troubled to apply elsewhere. Let me confess, also, that I had yet to turn 17 and opposite my beardless photograph in the high school yearbook was the damning phrase "takes life most seriously."

I wanted to be a physiologist and advanced courses in mathematics, organic and physical chemistry, and physics were needed for the physiology of the future. I spent endless hours in the chemistry and biological laboratories during term and at the Marine Biological Laboratories in Woods Hole during the summers, all leading toward publications in the *Journal of the American Chemical Society* and the *Biological Bulletin* while I was still an undergraduate. There was a flexible distribution requirement and I enjoyed taking small, relatively advanced courses in History and English rather than large survey courses. General Education came in 1948 and the Core Curriculum in 1979, but I'm still not convinced that "breadth" can be legislated by course requirements. More important, it seems to me, is the stimulation that comes from advisors and professors who are themselves broad people and who inspire students to look beyond their specialties. My freshman advisor gave chess parties in his rooms at Eliot House and he served fresh oysters with whiskey and the good advice to audit Kittredge's lectures on Shakespeare along with science courses for credit. At post-Lowell Harvard, breadth also comes from the students themselves who bring a cafeteria of interests and talents for all to share, including the faculty. Take a look at the bulletin boards of 1984.

I played in the Harvard Orchestra (the Pierian Sodality of 1808) as my father had done in 1896; he used to describe it in affectionate tones as the oldest and worst orchestra in the United States and it wasn't much better in my day. This brings me to the happy subject of music at Harvard and Radcliffe in 1984. I don't think that any field of endeavor at Harvard has undergone a comparable degree of improvement in the last 50 years. Excellent musicians abound amongst the undergraduates and there is keen competition for admission to the Harvard-Radcliffe Orchestra (HRO), the Bach Society, and other undergraduate chamber music groups. Sanders Theatre is packed at HRO concerts and many of the Houses are able to produce chamber music concerts and even operas of high quality. Programs include technically difficult works, both classical and contemporary, and the level of performance is truly remarkable.

My own proficiency on the cello has improved greatly since I played in the Harvard Orchestra 50 years ago but I wouldn't stand a chance at an audition today. The tables have turned and I can say with pride and delight in Harvard that things are so much *better* than they used to be. This month the HRO will embark on its second European tour, this time to include performances in Leningrad, Moscow, and other cities in the USSR as well as in London, Cambridge, Rotterdam, and Paris. The metamorphosis of music at Harvard has come about with the aid of quiet support from an administration that is sympathetic to the performing arts. Nevertheless, the faculty is not yet ready to grant academic credit for the performing arts and we have still to bridge the gap between the *Note and the Footnote.*

I did become a physiologist and after rotating through four universities (including Cambridge and University College, London) I returned "home" in 1946 to a faculty appointment in Physiology at the Harvard Medical School. In Europe, the preclinical sciences are taught in the undergraduate "collegiate" years and the physiological sciences are a major field of concentration for three years of undergraduate study. In the United States, however, the basic medical sciences, including Physiology, are part of the medical school curriculum. In 1946 there were only a few nonmedical "Ph. D." types on the faculty of Medicine and those of us who were in this category felt a strong allegiance to the Faculty of Arts and Sciences, which administered our graduate programs.

Revolutionary advances in medical science have since altered the balance; a vast research establishment has grown up within the great Harvard teaching hospitals as well as within the medical school proper. There are now hundreds of appointments of nonmedical scientists to the faculty of medicine and they could not possibly be accommodated within the Faculty of Arts and Sciences. Stellar research scientists, like performing artists, adorn the academic environment and may bring it fame but they can be difficult to assimilate into the essential raison d'etre of a medical school. Conflict between the vast and important research establishment in medicine and the goals of medical education is one of the most important problems that Harvard must face in the years to come and these problems are the subject of President Bok's 1983 Report to the Board of Overseers. In his words, reform of the medical curriculum " . . . may well turn out to be Harvard's most impressive innovation of the 1980s. "

John Pappenheimer '36 is George Higginson Professor of Physiology Emeritus. He has been on the faculties of Medicine and Arts and Sciences since 1946. In 1971 he was Overseas Fellow of Churchill College, Cambridge and in 1975–76 was Eastman Professor and Fellow of Balliol College, Oxford.

E . J . K A H N , J R .

Harvard Has Become My Friend

As I look back, dimly, on my four undergraduate years at Harvard, I observe with some embarassment that I took precious litle advantage then of the resources it spread lavishly before me. Oh, I was lucky enough to be able to listen to some of the towering professional voices of that era — Kittredge, Lowes, Whitehead, Merriman, young Finley — but the sorry truth is that my attentiveness sometimes lagged. I probably spent less time at Widener, moreover, than I did at the Wursthaus.

It was — in the middle 1930s — a time when the young could coast, slide, slither, get by. I went to some classes with some regularity, and I earned a respectable *cum* (which on reflection I doubt I deserved), but I was more of a diffident visitor to the old place, really, than a dedicated resident. And in the first 20 or so years after my graduation, what's more, I paid little heed to Harvard, except to take in an occasional football game. Yes, I did see the unforgettable 29-29 victory over Yale in 1968; what my wife, who'd never before been to a Harvard-Yale game, can't forget about that heady afternoon is that it is possible for a theoretically sane, mature male to lose his voice in 42 seconds.

Most people get more conservative as they grow older. Now that it has been nearly 50 years since as a wet-eared freshman I first climbed to my fourth-floor digs at Stoughton (when I'm strolling through the Yard these days, I am sometimes tempted to have another look at the old room, but that's a lot of stairs to mount merely to slake one's nostalgia), I find a radical change in my relationship to Harvard. I feel much closer to it, and much more involved in it, than I did when I was actually a full-time part of it.

Harvard Has Become My Friend

Having had two sons in the College may have made a difference, I suppose, but even before they were admitted, in the 1960s, I began to see the University in a new light. In childhood, one is apt to be thrown into the company of distant cousins whom one ignores; in adulthood one may discover that, quite apart from consanguinity, the cousins can become friends. Harvard has become my friend.

This late-blooming amity began, as I reconstruct it, in the 1950s, when research for a book I was working on drew me to the incomparable Theatre Collection at Widener. Next, in the following decade, I found myself writing a book about Harvard itself. I plunged giddily into the warm, accommodating Archives. Now, in the '80s, I am embarking on another research project that will require me to spend many hours, the happy chances are, in the library of the Botanical Museum. All I knew about the Botanical Museum while I was an undergraduate was that it housed Harvard's glass flowers, which were something one took visiting parents to gape at when one couldn't figure out anything else to do with them. I didn't even know then that the Museum *had* a library. Half a century later, I find that it does, and I find to my further surprise and delight that the whole building is run by a classmate of mine. We never met when we were undergraduates together. Just as well; I wasn't ready then. I am ready now — having, in the years since my 25th reunion, spent probably 10 times as many hours in Harvard libraries as I did when my family was paying tuition for my access to them. I guess I was a slow learner. In any event, I no longer feel detached, even uncomfortable, when confronted by Harvard's awesome offerings. I feel at home at Harvard.

E. J. Kahn '37, author, is a staff writer for The New Yorker *magazine and the author of two dozen books.*

GERARD PIEL

The Value of One Field of Learning

Owing to the accident of my employment, I have to suffer the embarrassment of being deferred to as a scientist. Such deference implies of course a gross misapprehension of science and its resolutely anti-authoritarian spirit. In my case, the deference is not only mistaken but misdirected — I took not a single course in science in college — and, what is worse, it slights my real academic credentials. In the Harvard Archives, I am inscribed as an historian.

While I succeeded in scanting Mr. Lowell's plans for my education on the distribution side, I am grateful to him and his colleagues for enforcing the proposition that undergraduate education should require concentration in one field of learning. The student, Mr. Lowell said, should come to "know in some field what the ultimate sources of opinion are, and how they are handled by those who profess it." To that end they provided tutorial instruction in the College, for mastery of a discipline in graduate education comes best by apprenticeship.

My experience of tutorial instruction in my field of concentration must be the model of what they had in mind; my children and their comtemporaries assure me they never had anything like it. To lift the sights of undergraduates; to prick the conscience of the faculty, especially in history, I record the story here.

My election of History as my field of concentration was also an accident. I came to Harvard with a near sight-reading pleasure in Latin. On this foundation, I first thought to concentrate in the Classics. Joshua Whatmough took me back to Square One, however, with his demand for tight parsing of every word and phrase in Plautus and Menander. Another course in my freshman year, the

A course in sociology, gave my education a more serious objective. (Sociology did not, of course, count toward the distribution requirement in science; nor is it the sort of science people have in mind when they call me a scientist.)

The stern discipline of Sociology was well incarnated in the lean and hungry graduate student to whom I reported as tutee. In his Calvinist view I was of the elect or not. There was only one way to find out; this was by the ordeal of sudden total immersion. He set me to reading the masters. The first was Emil Durkheim on *le Suicide*. I came to know intensely what this master meant by his concept of *anomie*. Werner Sombart, Karl Marx, and Max Weber came along more easily. Their concerted interest was the external world and a new idea for me: the process of history. In the reading and in my tutorial sessions I found my way to the conclusion that I had to learn some history before I could conjure with its process. As advertised by *History A*, with Roger Bigelow Merriman as principal advance man, history had become for me that year, in any case, a pleasurable distraction.

My retreat from sociology being one of the two possible outcomes of my tutor's experiment, there were no hard feelings. The defeat was all mine. My tutor went on to be Robert Merton, professor of the professors of sociology in our time, a fashioner of the intellectual apparatus of his science and founder of the sociology of science.

Starting into History in my junior year, I was impressed to find that my tutor was an Associate Professor. More important, as I soon discovered, he was Michael Karpovich. He had come out of history, himself. As youthful counsellor to the embassy of the Kerensky government, he had been marooned in Washington by the October Revolution. There he turned to the study of history. With him I had the privilege of sharing his effort to understand our world and time.

The reading Karpovich set me exceeded in pages and hours and diversity the combined assignments in all my courses. In fact my courses turned out to be appendages to the mainstream of my learning, which was my reading and my afternoons, once every two weeks, with Karpovich. Although Modern European History was my concentration within my concentration, he had me reading Edward Gibbon and Michael Rostovtzev on the decline of the Roman Empire as well as R. H. Tawney on the rise of capitalism and Count Witte on his attempt to start up industrial revolution in imperial Russia. The reading had an inner plan that became clear as it proceeded.

The first lesson I had to learn from Karpovich would seem easy enough. But it took a lot of reading to see that history is written by historians. From this, the other lessons followed. Karpovich taught me to look for the author's inexplicit premise, to assess his evidence, to examine my own premises, and to make the best of what each author had brought to hand.

Another tutor came out of history to replace Karpovich, on sabbatical, in my senior year. Dietrich Gerhardt was one of the scholars Mr. Conant rescued from the catastrophe of Nazism. With his benign encouragement I tackled a topic for my honors thesis too ambitious for any doctoral candidate; at least none had ever attempted it. This was the history of the French Socialist Party from its founding in the aftermath of the Commune to the outbreak of war in 1914. At my own carrel in the Widener stacks, which I acquired by acting like a doctoral candidate, I assembled the primary sources. My bibliography shows Widener held a` rich sampling of the fugitive, combative, and scholarly literature of the socialist movement in France, Germany, and England, including minutes of the national and international party congresses and files of the party newspapers. History was as generous as Widener: it endows my thesis with a plot. It was Jules Guesde, the doctrinaire sharpener of the class conflict, who entered the War Cabinet in 1914; it was Jean Jaures, for whom economic democracy was the necessary moral fulfillment of political democracy, who voted against the war credits (and was assassinated the next day).

To tutotial instruction in my field of concentration I owe such automomy as I possess. Because I came to know "the ultimate sources of opinion" in one field, even so briefly and long ago, I have some confidence in my ability to tell sense from nonsense.

Gerard Piel '37 is Editor and Publisher of Scientific American, *a former Overseer and former Radcliffe Trustee.*

Confession of a True Believer

I suppose it is possible that one could work for Harvard for 40 years and conclude that the effort had not been worthwhile. Yet I find it hard to imagine such a result — even among the humblest helper in the great enterprise. For me Harvard has been endlessly fascinating and there seems to be almost literally, something for everyone in the life of the University.

Harvard is an obsession not suddenly acquired. The University takes time to work its magic, and some are so constituted as never to respond willingly to its countless blandishments. On the other hand, over and over one hears older graduates express the belief that some aspect of Harvard had a strong influence on the goals and personal satisfactions of life; that the people who taught them were especially talented and devoted; and that there was something in the air — was it really purer, clearer, and more intoxicating in those student days? — that provided a standard against which all later life could be measured.

What the reminiscing alumni really mean is that they have made a personal Harvard a part of their lives, for the experience of Harvard is an intimate matter, depending as it does on the interaction of teacher and student, friend and friend, rival and role model, the influences of libraries, laboratories, theater, art, music, House activities, yearning and love, new impressions and fresh conclusions.

More than most I have benefited from that slow and captivating osmosis of Harvard's charm. Had my Harvard been only four college years in the mid 1930s, before World War II swept that Harvard almost completely away, it still would have been etched in memory as a period when an embarrassingly callow youth like myself, with limited background and horizons, grew up a little and, though he was recklessly wasteful of time and intellectual opportunity, still finds reason for gratitude. Gratitude for the constellation of great teachers then available to a concentrator in American history and literature; for the "gracious living" in Eliot House, where the morning sausages were served on individual slivers of toast, where faculty and students really did interact, where John Coddington's kind and easy-going ways set the tone for E-entry, where Fred Bissell of Dubuque spent countless hours getting an opinionated Miltonian to think seriously about Henry James, and where Harry Levin taught a spindly, kilted version of the courageous Earl of Douglas how to cross swords with royalty. Gratitude for the marginal publishing venture that was the *Advocate*, with its galaxy of literary stars — Cyrus Sulzberger, Gerard Piel, the younger Schlesinger, Jay Laughlin, and others. Gratitude even for the solitary winter and spring vacations when I gained admission to the Widener stacks and found amazing pleasure and satisfaction in the lonely job of creating two lengthy term papers on aspects of Jeffersonian democracy and on the African slave trade; for the excitement of meeting and hearing T. S. Eliot or Gertrude Stein at the Signet; and for the sweaty managerial privilege of moving bats and balls and more malodorous equipment in and out of Dillon every spring day in exchange for many languorous moments punctuated by the sound of horsehide against padded calfskin or Kentucky hickory, and the sight of laconic old Fred Mitchell throwing down his cap to protest a close call at first.

Yet with all these beguiling memories I can keenly recall how heartily I wanted to be rid of Harvard College, to put behind me the last exam — now that academic failure was no longer a peril — and be off with my love to our new life together and the experience of what the *Crimson* calls "the real world." Yet in three years I was back again, achieving thus quickly an ambition, hazily conceived

in senior year, to become the editorial proprietor of a small publication with its own special constituency. From then on, Harvard
was impossible to resist, its allure all the more potent because it
worked into the inner fiber of one who had the advantage of being
an observer as well as an actor. Fourteen years, less the years of
war, with the *Harvard Alumni Bulletin* in association with such literary
mentors as David McCord and David Bailey; 18 years as personal
assistant to President Pusey, one of the greatest teachers I have
known; and since then a kind of open-ended assignment to work
on historical projects relating to Harvard and make oneself useful
in a variety of other ways. Can I be forgiven for having become an
intense partisan of the Harvard experience and a true believer?

*William Bentinck-Smith '37, a writer and editor, is Senior Associate in the Office of the Secretary
to Harvard University. He was an Assistant to President Nathan Marsh Pusey and is former
editor of the Harvard Alumni Bulletin.*

Sitting on a Standing Committee

Assessing what Harvard/Radcliffe means to me is not quite the simple task I envisioned when I first happily agreed to do it.

Part of the difficulty I found is that I have been connected with Harvard/Radcliffe now for a period spanning 48(!) years in such a variety of ways that I have had to think through which experiences have had the greatest impact, or whether my feelings are, in fact, the cumulative effect of all of them. It has been important, too, to sort out fact from fantasy, reality from romanticism, and truth from fiction in order to think honestly about *why* I have maintained this long-lasting relationship when the "old school tie" does not seem to hold that much significance for many other Black graduates.

Certainly, these past five years as an Overseer have provided a new and very different way of looking at the University. When Mike Bessie called to ask if I would stand for nomination, he did not overstate the case when he advised that it would be a very demanding job. Yet, there is no question that sitting on Standing Committees and Visiting Committees provides a deeper respect for the scope of the institution as a whole with new insights into *how* the University functions and *why*. And that view is very different from that which I had as a member of the Associated Harvard Alumni, or as a member of the Radcliffe Alumnae Board during the early days of merger-nonmerger negotiations, or as an undergraduate from 1934 to 1938.

Memories of those earliest days are blurred. I listen and wonder now when I hear Radcliffe women speaking about their mind-stretching experiences of contact with the Harvard "greats," the excitement and stimulation provided by their tutors, and the thrill of it all. For me, I guess that the period was primarily just a rite of passage; and I lacked the sophistication and aggressiveness to reach out on my own to take greater advantage of what Harvard/Radcliffe offered. Sad to say, tutorial was a disaster, and if there were other individual guidance and support systems available, I never found them.

Coming out of a Black upper middle-class family where I was constantly reminded of who I was and what was expected of me, I do not recall that "finding myself" was a big agenda item. However, having graduated as valedictorian from an excellent New Jersey suburban high school, having known from the third grade that I was "going to Radcliffe," and having been accepted under the "Highest Seventh Plan" without examination, I did have to handle the shock of two A's and two D's as grades for my freshmen year. That undoubtedly contributed to my growth.

As a Romance Languages major, I remember the lectures and classes with Professors Mercier and Allard, but it was exposure to Pitirim Sorokin and his brilliant young "section man," Robert Merton, which sparked the interest that sent me to the stacks on my first independent search for more information. Even more than that, it was also the start of my search for what was to become my proper niche in life.

Of course, there were the friends I made, the girls in Whitman Hall with whom I shared the day-to-day dormitory living, the anxieties at exam time, the joy and heartbreak of love affairs, and the eternal gossipy night sessions. Initially, there had been a skirmish with the Radcliffe administration around whether or not I, as a Black student, would be "happy" living in a dormitory. That battle was won for me by a strong, determined, protective mother and the three years I spent in Whitman were relatively free from overt brushes with prejudice and discrimination . . . but then, I *was* the only Black student there. I do look back with some amusement at Jennie (not her real name), the little girl from the South who wailed in all seriousness about wishing she could take me home with her to prove to her doubting family and friends that I *did* exist!

There are other memories, warm ones such as being invited to speak at 1938's 15th and 25th Reunions (on combining career and marriage) and being selected in 1964 for the Radcliffe Alumnae Achievement Award. There was also my daughter's wedding day in Memorial Chapel in 1966 and her graduation in 1967. Nor can I ignore the fact that scattered among my family's relatives by blood and by marriage are 10 Harvard/Radcliffe degrees, including a third generation one held by Frank M. Snowden III in a direct line through his maternal grandfather, Dr. Leslie Pinckney Hill and his father, Frank M. Snowden, Jr. '32, A.B., M.A., Ph.D.

Consequently, as I look back over all of these years, it does not seem at all illogical that Harvard/Radcliffe has continued to play an important part in my life. Yet, in all of this, there is something of a love-hate relationship. In more cynical moments, I have wondered whether my living in such close geographical proximity to Harvard has played any part in the rather persistent way in which I have been pulled into its orbit. Dealing with the complexities of claims to "pure meritocracy" at the University does pose problems and I can empathize with those Black students today who are still struggling with them.

I am still struggling, too, because as an activist and a feminist, I become impatient with the slow pace at which Harvard works to combat racism and sexism within its own structure. I am hard put to maintain the long view when every day of my life at Freedom House I am forced to deal with their deadly effects.

Yet, despite the fact that there is still such a long way to go, I am conscious of the debt I owe Harvard/Radclilffe in terms not only of helping to refine an intellectual curiosity and a willingness to face change which keeps life for me a continuing, unfolding adventure, but also for contributing to the relative ease with which I have been able to move effectively in two worlds. The prestige of the institution which I carry with me has opened many doors and has enabled me, in concert with my husband, to utilize it for the benefit and in the interest of the Black communities of Boston and environs to which we pledged our allegiance over 33 years ago.

Muriel Sutherland Snowden '38 is a member of the Board of Overseers, and co-founder and co-director of Freedom House, Inc. of Roxbury, Massachusetts.

THEODORE H. WHITE
A Mirror of American History

Two years after I graduated from Boston Public Latin School, confused, angry, and on my way to nowhere, Harvard College gave me a scholarship of $220 and the Borrough's Newsboy Foundation added another $180, the exact amount needed for a year's tuition at Harvard. So it was that in September 1934, I emerged from the subway exit in the Square and faced what remains in my fond eye the most beautiful campus in America, the Harvard Yard. If there is any one place that mirrors better all American history, I do not know of it.

I arrived at Harvard the year after Dr. Conant, who wanted to make Harvard something more than a New England school. He wanted its faculty to be more than a gentlemen's club of courtly, learned men, wanted its student body to be national in origin. Excellence was his goal, and his insistence on it made Harvard the most competitive school in American scholarship, a meritocracy in which students and professors vied for honors with little mercy or kindness. As we squatted on the floor of the Freshman Union, he told us what a university was: a place for free minds. "If you call everyone to the right of you a Bourbon, and everyone to the left of you a Communist, you'll get nothing out of Harvard," he said. And he explained that what we would get out of Harvard was what we could take from it ourselves; Harvard was open, so — go seek.

My approach to Harvard and its riches was that of a looter. Not only were there required courses to be attended, but there were courses given by famous men, lectures open to all, where no one guarded the entry. But it was a required course, *History I*, that exposed me to perhaps the most colorful character on Harvard's then vivid faculty of characters. "Frisky" Merriman believed history was story — thus, entertainment.

"Frisky" stretched the story from the Age of the Antonines to the Treaty of Versailles — all 1,800 years. His course was like an express train, pausing only at major stops on the track of history, and always, there would be "Frisky," like a conductor, calling the next stop and ultimate arrival, closing his lecture with "Unity, gentlemen, unity!" Europe, he held, had sought the long lost unity Rome had given it 2,000 years ago as a man seeks to recapture a dream.

The first direction in which *History I* led came by mechanical accident. It led across a corridor in Boylston Hall — to China. It was easier to study in the empty library of the Harvard-Yenching Institute than the *History I* reading room. If I was bleary reading about medieval trade or the Reformation, I could pick Chinese volumes off the shelves — volumes on fine rice paper, blue-bound, bamboo-hooked. My eyes rested on the scrolls of calligraphy on the walls, and I began to feel at home. I chose Chinese History and Language as my sophomore field of concentration.

A more dangerous choice I never made. In those days, the Chinese department at Harvard had the standards of the Emperor Ch'ien-lung laced with a dash of sadism. To learn the language, one was required to pound each character into the mind by sheer force of recall, as one pounds nails into a board. I was put on notice of dismissal within six weeks of joining the course; but since my scholarship and hence my survival at Harvard was at stake, I studied until one, two, or three in the morning. I survived with a gratifying A.

Harvard's History Department offered more than American and Chinese history. It offered a banquet of invitations to the past, of famous courses, of byways and coves and special delights of learning. There was Professor Crane Brinton, cynical, caustic, disdainful of all morals, who claimed Talleyrand as his own particular hero;

Arthur Schlesinger, Sr., a magnificent teacher; and Paul Buck. There was Abbott Payson Usher, whose course taught the way men make things and traded things, and that history rests on how they manage the manufacturing and exchange of goods. He simply took all my previous ideas, shook them apart gently, then taught me how facts and large affairs arrange themselves in connections that made history seem like intellectual detective work.

Yet the teacher who, more than any other spun me off into history as a life calling, was a young man who arrived in my junior year: John King Fairbank, later to become the greatest historian of America's relations with China. He was on trial at Harvard, both as a tutor and Orientalist; since I was the only undergraduate majoring in Chinese studies, I was assigned to him as tutee.

It was not only that I was invited to my first tea party at his home, learning to balance a teacup properly. It was his absolute devotion to forcing my mind to think that speeded the change in me. He would make the hardest work a joy, and his monthly assignments were written with a skill and personal attention that no tutor at Harvard, or anywhere else, today gives to his students.

In my senior year, young John Fairbank was allowed to teach a course on China from the death of Ch'ien-lung to our times. It was a magnificent series of lectures, ground-breaking in intellectual patterns. It inflamed my itch to be off, away and out — to China, where the story lay.

Everything had come together in those last few months at Harvard. It was reading Chinese, steeping myself in history, writing about the Twenty-one Demands, slowly swinging in my politics from Socialist to hushed approval of Roosevelt's New Deal, concealing from friends that I was participating in ROTC exercises. My mother and sister came in by streetcar and subway to watch me graduate, and found nothing at all noteworthy in the program's statement that I had graduated *summa cum laude*. That is what they had expected ever since I had entered the Boston Latin School.

Theodore H. White '38, is a former war correspondent, Pulitzer Prize-winner, author of The Making of the President series, and former Overseer.

"Depart Better to Serve Thy Country"

Looking back over 40 years, I suppose my most vivid impressions are of the healthy skepticism implanted by most of the Harvard faculty — learning how to think, having all your assumptions challenged and being required either to support them or abandon them under Harvard's withering intellectual crossfire. These, I might add, are scarcely negligible training aids for one contemplating public life!

My first impression on arriving in the fall of 1934 was that of total chaos. I had graduated in the top seven of San Francisco's Polytechnic High School, and thus was spared the entrance board examinations. But the standard work load at Harvard was enormously heavier than anything I'd experienced. At school, 20 lines of Latin had been a massive assignment; at Harvard, our instructor, an Englishman on loan from Cambridge University, said because we were "so busy" settling in — he'd only give us 200 lines for the first night.

Most of my first year was spent catching up. I took *Government I*, Latin and, because you had to have both ancient and modern languages, *two* German courses to get these out of the way. The only two C's I received at Harvard were in that double German course, and I was happier to have them than any other grade I received. I lived with my sophomore brother in fine, panelled rooms at the top of the Union: very convenient when the Yard was deep in snow. Moreover, the view was splendid. I'll never forget when Army played Harvard that first fall and the long gray lines of

West Point cadets filed into the Union, wheeled and sat down as one. The contrast with the Harvard students — who slumped over the table — was impressive, and not all that much in Harvard's favor.

I was never a major athlete. Freshmen had to learn to swim 50 yards in the pool, but I'd had punctured eardrums and kept getting ear infections. So I never learned to swim. I ran a bit and tossed the javelin. I got German measles, along with about everyone else, and met practically the entire editorial board of the *Crimson* at the Stillman infirmary: John B. Bowditch, Charles M. Storey, Jr., Arthur A. Ballantine, Jr., Henry V. Poor, Michael Bessie and others. They seemed to enjoy life so much that I decided to try out for the *Crimson*.

About 70 of us started. Every so often some would be cut, spurring the remainder to frantic endeavor. I was given various assignments — sports, faculty appointments, movie and theater reviews — but we were also expected to come up with features of our own. I managed to interview Colonel Theodore Roosevelt, Jr., Harold Laski, and Tallulah Bankhead. She was my big, feature triumph.

Laski refused to be interviewed, but I got into his first lecture and at the end, when he took questions, I used some of his answers to write up an "interview." Tallulah Bankhead was opening at the Colonial in, I believe, *Dark Victory*. Backstage, she was horrified when I confessed I had not seen the play — she wanted praise. The problem was, I did not have the money for theater tickets and the *Crimson* had no funds for expenditures as unnecessary as that.

The *Crimson* was a tough taskmaster. You'd begin around two or three in the afternoon and work straight through till nearly midnight. The *Crimson* could not buy the UP services, but the *Boston Herald* let us have their carbons. When it was my turn, I'd take the subway to Park Square at 11 at night, so as to get the latest news into our morning paper, walk down Washington Street to the

Herald, and race back to Cambridge just in time to turn selected items into "News Briefs" for a page one column. I was also writing a column called "Along the Atlantic Seaboard" for a San Francisco magazine. Mostly, I'd "adopt" it from the *New York Herald Tribune*. By spring of my sophomore year I was elected assistant managing editor and in my junior year, managing editor and then president along with Morris "Mo" Earle. There were two presidents for each class in those days. My biggest innovation was to change the constitution — after Mo had had his turn — to have only one president for each class, and in 1939 Cleveland Amory became the first president to serve the full year.

I majored in Government, completing my requirements in junior year and concentrating thereafter on my chief interest, English history. I'll never forget my horror when the professor in one of my English history classes, Wilbur Cortez Abbott, sniffed that the American victims of the 1770 Boston massacre were nothing but "a bunch of hired ruffians who sent down and shot up the regular British troops."

I was elected to Phi Beta Kappa and became treasurer of the Student Council with Frank Keppel as president. I was in Dunster House for the three years after my freshman year at the Union.

I won the John L. Saltonstall prize and the Lionel de Jersey Harvard prize, endowed by one of the few traceable descendants of John Harvard. I had decided to go straight into the Harvard Law School, so I declined it, but, looking back, I know it was a major mistake. It would have given me a year in John Harvard's rooms at Emmanuel College, Cambridge, with no specific academic requirements and paid travel on the continent during the long vacations. I would have seen and experienced much that was beautiful but later destroyed during World War II.

As for politics, I did play around a little with the small Young Republican group, and I well remember Professor Holcombe in government classes, ending each hour with: "Now we'll hear from

Weinberger, our Republican." The undergraduates in Government and Economics were overwhelmingly pro-FDR Democrats although the rest of the college was generally Republican, to the extent they were politically interested at all. I'd give the Conservative viewpoint, the bell would ring and I'd move out to continue my missionary work elsewhere. I remember betting my classmate, Ben Welles, some vast sum on the Roosevelt-Landon race in 1936. This was right after the 1936 Republican Convention, where I served as an usher. I assigned more importance to the cheers at the Convention than to public opinion generally. I lost, of course, and decided never again to bet on politics!

During my three years in Law School, I was hired as a proctor in Matthews Hall in the Yard, and so kept up the close association with the College I have missed ever since.

The meaning of Harvard to me was always best expressed by the statement chiseled into the top of the gate leading into the Yard from Mass. Avenue across from Plympton Street — "Enter to Grow in Wisdom," and as you left the Yard, on the opposite side — "Depart Better to Serve Thy Country and Thy Kind."

Caspar Weinberger '38, JD '41, is U.S. Secretary of Defense, former Secretary of Health, Education and Welfare, former Director of Bechtel Corporation, and former president of the Harvard Crimson.

JOHN F. KENNEDY

Sower of the Seed

Professor George Lyman Kittredge is supposed to have stopped in
the Harvard Yard one day, pointed to the Widener Library, and
remarked that every other building could burn to the ground, but
if the Library continued to stand, "we should still have a University."

I share Professor Kittredge's admiration for the Library. But I am
inclined to think that even the Library could be devoured in a
general conflagration and the essence of Harvard would endure if
teachers like Kittredge and his fellows survived. For the real meaning of Harvard is not in the buildings or the Library, however
important their supporting functions may be; it is in the teachers
and the students and the interrelationship between them. The
teachers, not the Library, serve as the organ of memory, distilling
the knowledge of the past, and, in the words of Woodrow Wilson,
transmitting to the future the best traditions of the State.

I have known many great teachers at Harvard, many who excelled in showing the enchantment of thought to young men who,
in this springtime of youth, were more enchanted with life itself.
But the one teacher known to generations of Harvard students who
stands out in my memory and personal affections is Arthur Holcombe. Under his direction in a course in American Government,
I discovered for the first time the distractions of the Congressional
Record, as I studied for one term the rise and eventual political
extinguishment of an obscure Republican Congressman from up-
state New York.

But Professor Holcombe's greatest impact was not in his erudition
but in his personality and character. Dispassionate, reserved, self-
restrained, without illusions yet persistently idealistic, he was ex-

traordinarily well equipped with qualities and principles to meet his responsibilities as a teacher and as a citizen. He taught and inspired my father. Forty years later he taught and inspired, with equal brilliance, my younger brother. To them, to me, to all his students, he set a standard to which in later life we could repair.

Shortly after the 1946 election he remarked to me with unconcealed pride: "I had the pleasure on election day of voting for three of my former students — one for Senator, one for Governor and one for Congressman — and they were all elected." It did not matter to him that the party labels were different; they had been his students, they were graduates of Harvard, he respected their capabilities and motives — and that was enough.

I trust that fire is not about to envelop the Harvard Yard, and that Widener Library will be standing long after all the present faculty and students are gone. But I am even more confident that the spirit of the Holcombes and the Kittredges and all the rest will endure even longer. And Harvard will endure with it.

John F. Kennedy received the degree of S.B. from Harvard in 1940 and the honorary LL.D. in 1956. He served his country as Congressman, Senator, and President. He served his college as an Overseer.

A L A N   J A Y   L E R N E R

Form and Content

It was unseasonably warm for late October. There was no tang, no trace of the world-famous New England autumn in the air. I was in Boston, opening a new musical play I had written. The heavy limpness that hung over Beacon Hill was easily matched by the two acts I had put on display in the theatre. For a writer there is no feeling of exposure, no naked defenselessness that equals standing at the end of a dark aisle and listening to one's words being said. If they reach a common heart there is no greater joy, no relief as boundless. If they miss their mark, there is no humiliation, no loneliness as devastating. That October night of 1951 my words were missing marks with spectacular proficiency.

When the curtain came down, I fled the lobby to avoid the comments of the audience. The theatre is the one place you can hear silence, and I had heard their comments while the curtain was up. Backstage, the actors regarded me one-part hopefully — hopeful that I would find a solution for their mutual embarrassment — and one-part with the respectful disdain with which a child looks at a parent who has given him the wrong present for Christmas. I left the theatre, and more for escape than any other reason, I drove to Cambridge.

It was the first time that I had returned to Harvard since that June afternoon eleven years before, when I closed my trunk, said an unsentimental goodbye to sundry friends and went taxiing off to Back Bay, without so much as a single long, lingering look at those memory-packed buildings I was leaving behind. Until then, the last day — the last four years — I had spent there had not crossed my mind more than half a dozen times. But suddenly, that night, probably because the feeling of separateness was acute, those four years came rushing back, and for the first time, what they had meant, what Harvard had meant, became a clear and conscious part of my life.

What passed before my mind's eye was not the crisp November Saturday afternoons and the excitement of a whistle blowing, not the Pudding shows, which I loved so much, not the parties that became parties unexpectedly. All of that and more like it is a part of college days, and was a part of mine, too. Nor was it, oddly enough, the awareness of that residue of education they call knowledge.

No. In the shadows of those dark buildings, I sensed for the first time that here I had spent a part of my life that had form and content, a form and content as perfectly wrought as a work of art. Those four years had a unity of time and place that was college, and a content that was Harvard. It was the only period of living I shall ever know that had a beginning, a middle and an end, within whose invisible boundaries I worked, played, knew joy, sadness, and felt a part. It would never happen to me again, not professionally, in love, with children or home. For from that June afternoon on, events started bumping into events, emotions spilled over into emotions, and nothing ever again would precisely begin or precisely end. Yet discovering it did not fill me with regret. Instead, understanding it gave me a jolt of happiness for what I had had, and I left the Yard refreshed and at peace.

It would be pleasant to be able to say that after that walk I struck a new well of inspiration and in no time at all the audience was beside itself with glee. Not at all. The play was not very good and never got to be very good. But ever since that night, Harvard has been firmly etched in my heart and mind. It was as if, after eleven years, I had finally spent my last night at school.

Alan Jay Lerner received the A.B. degree from Harvard in 1940. He has written the libretti for "Brigadoon," "Paint Your Wagon" and "My Fair Lady."

BARBARA MILLER SOLOMON

Happy in Our Own Environment

Crossing the Charles River in the fall of 1936, I could not know that I was never to return to Boston to live, but that I would make Cambridge my home. I had resisted going to Radcliffe, where it was evident that my father wanted me to enroll. After missing the College Boards because of a "strep" throat, my destiny was set when Dean Bernice Brown Cronkhite telephoned my mother and said, "Tell Barbara not to worry — Radcliffe has admitted her." Although Smith and Wellesley followed with letters of admission the next week, I rationalized to myself that Radcliffe had asked me first.

At the opening tea to welcome freshmen, I discovered that there was another girl with my name, another Barbara Miller. She and I both survived our identity crisis and decided over tea and cucumber sandwiches that we liked each other. So I entered the small, precious community of Radcliffe students.

Our college had two overlapping spheres: one occupied by those living in the dormitories, and one made up of those living at home. Although half the college commuted from nearby suburbs and towns, extracurricular activities as well as classes brought us into real communication with one another from the two spheres. I wanted quite simply to know everyone in the College, classmates from California, North Dakota, Missouri, Indiana, Ohio, as well as New York and Massachusetts. (I don't recall any Southerners nor did I recognize then the social limits of our regional differences.) Above all, Radcliffe has meant friendships with other women — many lifelong. Years later, despite time and distance, we talk when we meet as if we were still undergraduates.

Paradoxically, in the midst of the Depression, we "dorm" students lived in a well-appointed world where maids announced gentlemen callers. I thoroughly enjoyed the genteel way of life—being served meals and after-dinner coffee in the living room, tea by candlelight in the Agassiz cafeteria, and all with talk and more talk.

But we were also very much young women of the post-Prohibition generation — enjoying our first cocktails at St. Clair's in the Square, and drinking beer on the backstairs of the dormitory. And alas, all too often we regarded smoking as a measure of our independence and sophistication.

The heads of the dormitories (called Hall mistresses), the deans at Fay House, and the President all represented authority; I wanted to keep them at a distance. We undergraduates did not think of them as role models, nor did we know that term. Yet we were in awe of "Miss Comstock," Radcliffe's president, and knew even then that we had been touched by a vanishing breed of female educator. Ada Comstock had an extraordinary presence — she radiated dignity, strength and decisiveness.

My one coeducational experience occurred in 1938 with the appointment of Mlle. Nadia Boulanger as Visiting Lecturer in Music at Radcliffe. Ada Comstock had raised the money to pay Boulanger with the approval of Harvard's Music Department when it could not afford to fund her. I can still see the Fay House auditorium jammed with women and men, undergraduates and graduate students taking advantage of this unique opportunity to study with the renowned French woman, the teacher of so many modern composers. For a novice like me, her course was a turning point in learning how to hear and understand the sounds of early and modern music.

For the most part, we at Radcliffe were supremely happy in our own environment. For us, Harvard remained "the other." Most of us felt no institutional connection to it; we did not think of ourselves as second-class citizens in the University; instead, we enjoyed our own collegiate traditions and activities. Associations with Harvard came through individual professors and through our male friends. Though classes were separate, we had our share of Harvard men (some suitors, like mine, we married). We were not bothered by the fact that some Harvard faculty members would not teach at Radcliffe; but we loved those who did.

Memorable in my education was Tutorial at the Radcliffe Tutorial House, where faculty and students shared coffee and chatted before and after the weekly session. My tutor in Greek History and Literature, Sterling Dow, introduced me to the study of gravestones, and thus I learned that artifacts were as much a part of ancient history as the Iliad and the Greek lyric poets whom I was reading with classicist John Finley. The very different perspectives of these two young instructors laid a groundwork that later I found of value in studying the history of American civilization.

The undergraduate course of study was as demanding as it was exciting. I wanted to be an "all-round" student and made a point of not being a "grind." Nevertheless, I took particular delight when in the senior year I was assigned a stall in Widener Library, where women were generally forbidden to tarry. I fell in love with the stacks, and working there became a permanent addiction.

Clearly Radcliffe had opened new possibilities, intellectually and personally. Although many of us did not know what we wanted to do after graduation, we were confident that we could do anything, once we made up our minds.

Barbara Miller Solomon '40, PhD '53, is Senior Lecturer on History and Literature and on the History of American Civilization. Formerly Associate Dean of Radcliffe College, she became the first woman Assistant Dean at Harvard College. Her writings include Ancestors and Immigrants, Pioneers in Service, *and the forthcoming* In the Company of Educated Women.

ELLIOT L. RICHARDSON
City Upon a Hill

Harvard is critical, curious, skeptical, tolerant, principled. Harvard is as old as antiquity and as new as tomorrow's Nobel Prize-winning discovery. Harvard is above all humane, and its humanity rests on deep respect and high hope for all human beings.

Is this trite? Banal? The people who are Harvard are not likely to think so. They know that whatsoever is true, lovely, or of good report is always in danger of being taken for granted. They know that institutions that are taken for granted are doomed to wither and die.

At Harvard, the renewal and increase of strength come from the teaching and research of scholars whose gifts have been painstakingly sought out and patiently encouraged. They come from students whose curiosity and creativity are stimulating to their teachers as well as to each other. They come from libraries and laboratories; dining-rooms and dormitories; lecture halls and playing-fields; the *Lampoon*, the *Crimson*, and the *Advocate* — and, in my day, especially the *Lampoon*. And they come, in generous measure, from a host of loyal alumni.

All of us who love Harvard — and most of those who don't — identify Harvard with excellence. Not that Harvard always and uniformly achieves it. That is not possible. We identify Harvard with excellence, rather, in the sense that Harvard always and invariably *seeks* excellence — which is to say that Harvard seeks to *excel*. Harvard is seldom No. 2 and will never settle for trying harder.

What Harvard stands for is more important to me than what it is or what it has done. Harvard for me is John Winthrop's city upon a hill: the eyes of all people are upon it.

This means, I suppose, that my deepest feeling toward Harvard is not gratitude (though my indebtedness is incalculable) but pride. And if it be a sin to be proud of Harvard, I am the most offending soul alive.

Elliot L. Richardson '41, LL.B. '47, former Overseer, is Senior Resident Partner in the Washington law firm Milbank, Tweed, Hadley & McCloy. He has served as U.S. Secretary of Health, Education and Welfare; Secretary of Defense; and Secretary of Commerce. He is former Ambassador to the Court of St. James.

Adult Education

Harvard has come to mean a variety of quite disparate qualities to me. First, there was the Harvard I attended. Those remembrances are blurred not only because they occurred a long time ago, but also because they were not a very sharply etched experience. My life did not appear to be very much affected by what I learned there, nor by the people I met there.

I enjoyed my encounters with some great teachers, but seem to have better memories of locker rooms than classrooms. For many years I saw relatively little of any classmates. Nor in truth did I feel much loyalty, much generosity or much admiration. Harvard probably was more important to me than I realized but such was my perception.

The first change in that point of view came after a meeting in New York for The Program for Harvard College in 1958. I recall vividly driving home after seeing a Harvard movie and hearing the requisite speeches, and telling my wife that I was unmoved by the evening's events, and had a number of reservations about the snobbishness and fatuousness that permeated much of Harvard. Her reply was that, whether such an evaluation was fact or fiction, if I were going to give support to college education, Harvard was where it would logically go; she had no picture of me supporting Yale or Princeton in a big way.

That was the beginning of an involvement that has included membership on my Class's 25th Reunion committee, being an elected Director of the Associated Harvard Alumni, Chairman of the Harvard College Fund, twice an Overseer, President of the

Harvard Club of New York, Trustee of Radcliffe, and Co-Chairman of The Harvard Campaign.

My "second" attendance at Harvard has spanned more than 15 years, has been more intense, and has made a far more lasting impression than my three-and-a-half-year first tour.

Harvard, as a center for intellectual and scholarly endeavor, bringing together, as it does, a larger conglomeration of brilliant and innovative people than any other single institution of which I have any knowledge, makes a very great difference in the way this country functions. To the degree that we solve the myriad problems we face in the present-day world — whether dealing with science and society; with ordering the relationships between nations; in understanding better the physical structure of life; with the motivation of humans toward a higher ethic — all those and many other problems will be solved by the Harvards of the world or not at all. Harvard's faculty and students both have an extraordinary involvement in all facets of our society. We who passed through those gates are privileged to belong to quite a special club.

Spending time seeing the innards of Harvard is revealing. Many of its most valuable qualities have negative side effects and in some cases can do harm to the institution if not actively guarded against. Any organization we get to know very well reveals its weaknesses, and Harvard is not perfect. Excellence can breed arrogance, and Harvard has been prolific.

Success may build ego and an unwillingness to admit weakness or error. Elitism nurtures the image of infallibility and self-righteousness, though the recognition that humans are unequal is, to me, refreshing.

But those same qualities, good and bad, are part of the amalgam that makes Harvard a very vital and creative and fascinating and important place.

Learning about it has enhanced my sensitivity to the role of intellectuals in our world and to the great responsibility that leadership has in fulfilling its own manifest destiny. The obligations that accompany excellence are very great, not only in quality of performance, but also in quality of character. Harvard must continue to strive for both.

Walter "Bill" Rothschild '42 was Co-Chairman of The Harvard Campaign, the $350-million fund drive, twice a member of the Harvard Board of Overseers, and formerly a Radcliffe College trustee. He is also Chairman of the Board of St. Luke's Roosevelt Hospital Center.

JUSTIN KAPLAN

Sinking and Swimming

The last peacetime entering class before World War II encountered a different Harvard and Cambridge from their present counterparts. If the Square was not quite the ugliest spot on the face of God's earth, as William Dean Howells remembered it from the 1880s, it was still a contender. With the exception of bookstores lining Massachusetts Avenue and Boylston Street, the rest of Cambridge was a dingy remainder of the industrial revolution. Southwest winds blowing across the Charles from the Brighton slaughterhouses added flavors of sweet decay to Cambridge's normal fly-ash and chemical pollution. For sport one could stone rats in the city dump located on the river bank below Henry James's grave in Cambridge Cemetery.

Harvard College itself was smaller but also more formal, physically luxurious (waitresses, maid service, single suites) but spiritually spartan. "Combined instruction" with Radcliffe came in during the war, out of necessity, not principle, and for many of us changed for the better the entire idea of education. That is another story. The place was served by an administrative skeleton, instead of today's well-fleshed, rather overweight body, some harried proctors, a tiny, unarmed constabulary in civilian clothes whose main function was to keep high-spirited students out of the clutches of the city police, and a medical staff of simple bonesetters and pill-rollers for whom urinalysis was still an outpost on the frontier of diagnostics. As for psychological counselling, study counselling, and other such support services and safety nets, there simply was none of this to speak of, beyond a few sympathetic but overworked tutors. The system, or lack of it, cruel or indifferent by current standards, produced an alarming casualty rate of washouts and suicides. In place of parietal care, however, the college offered students a nurturing and challenging mental atmosphere along with the privilege of being entirely, although often miserably, on their own to sink or swim.

For withdrawn and vulnerable newcomers, life at Harvard, especially in the dark period following Pearl Harbor, could easily conduce to fits of gloom so intense that they were delicious, like terror, and enhanced consciousness. After a year or two of floundering in the sciences and a semester's leave of absence in the Southwest, I decided that I might as well indulge myself and drown happy, in language.

The choice might not have been so easy in a less indifferent and therefore less trusting, more parentally and academically protective institution. Literature did not make much career sense in wartime, or in peacetime either, for that matter, but this hardly seemed important: all spring broke loose, year-round, and even unlovely Cambridge proved hard to leave when the time came for leaving. A few memorable teachers, among them F. O. Matthiessen, suggested that there was a vital link between literature and experience. Through no fault of theirs, this lesson took many post-college years to penetrate. Still, if a whale-ship was, as Herman Melville said, his Harvard, I suppose I could say that Harvard was my whale-ship.

Justin Kaplan '45, Pulitzer Prize-winning biographer and national Book Award winner for his book on Mark Twain is a distinguished biographer. He is married to the novelist, Anne Bernays. They live in Cambridge.

MAXINE KUMIN

Blessed Be the Tie that Binds

To have come to a time of life when reminiscences arrive unbidden is to have dessert thrust alongside the meatloaf, catching you in mid-forkful. When I read about Brodsky and Sokolov, Sinyavsky and Solzhenitsyn writing in exile in their mother tongue, zealous to preserve it, I remember my struggle to acquire the Russian language, a process accentuated with proverbs.

It was 1943. Harvard had initiated, for the duration at least, joint classes with Radcliffe. Cambridge was crammed with khaki and blue serge. The jolly-ups were full of Ninety Day Wonders. As part of ASTP — the Army Student Training Program — the University was offering for the first time ever an intensive course in the Russian language.

I enrolled along with one other 'Cliffie. (*Two in a troika can never be lonely.*) We met with 28 Army privates at eight o'clock in the morning six days a week in a varnished brown room in the old brown bastion of Sever Hall. Thanks to Army discipline, no cuts were allowed. Our instructor, a mild-mannered linguistic genius, sat informally on the edge of the desk and addressed us by our somewhat capriciously assigned Russian names. Mine was Makseena Petrovna.

On the first day of class we were to memorize the 32-letter Russian alphabet, full of bewilderingly familiar but misleading signposts. On the second day, still reeling from the effects of printing backwards *R*'s which answered to *ya*'s and mastering a vowel which is sounded as *you* but to this day looks to me like the trademark for H-O Oats, we undertook to learn the symbols for cursive writing — 32 new curves, hooks, and flourishes.

A horse has four legs, yet he stumbles. Onward we slogged, dutifully plodding through four hours of assigned homework nightly. We two 'Cliffies studied together to absorb the conjugation of tortuous Russian verbs, the declension of masculine and feminine nouns, the cases taken by a rich variety of prepositions. Alas, every logical grammatical rule has its illogical but inexorable exception. The evenings were not long enough. At 10 p.m. we signed out — obedient to the parietals of yesteryear — and resumed our briefings in a delicatessen no wider than a diner that had recently opened on Mass. Avenue.

The proprietor of the Midget Restaurant, the late Al Kagan, an amiable, balding gentleman, seemed to have no objection to our lingering in a booth until closing time over cups of black coffee. There we attacked the enemy in the present, the compund future, the imperative, and the subjunctive. We fixed the position of the imperfective past gerund as a verbal adverb. We mouthed the strange vowels, we contorted our palates with hard and soft con-sonants, impaled the elusive shifting accents, solved the riddle of the genitive, and swept down on the mobility of *o* and *e* in the nominative singular.

One night *gospodin* Kagan overheard us toiling through the conjugation of the two forms of the verb *to go* — for the Russian makes an explicit distinction between motion on foot or in a vehicle — and offered to help us. Blessed be the tie that binds! None is so strong as the mutual shoelace of the spoken word. Here stood our angel, swathed in his butcher's apron, beneficent sharer of his native tongue.

We were well-fed pupils. With the coffee there now appeared from time to time corned beef on seeded roll. *(To break bread is to break the sword.)* I came to conquer the neuter declension with herring in sour cream and the ethical dative with pumpernickel. Our mentor lavished us with proverbs. At closing time we favored one (of course it loses its rhyme in translation) as poignant as Anna Karenina herself: *Goodnight, lovely ladies. There is never enough time for kissing.*

Well, the Midget Restaurant is no longer the Midget Restaurant. Today it's the Ground Round with parking lot and cocktail lounge and private banquet facilities. I never achieved my goal, which was to read Dostoievski in the original. All that I learned in that breakneck excursion through *Slavic One* has rusted away, leaving me the bare I-beams of a few proverbs, four dozen nouns, a phrase here and there in the UN's televised speeches, and a crystalline lyric of Pushkin's which begins: "I loved you once . . . "

And my Radcliffe friend in the lost war with the tongue of the boyars and comrades? Does she too remember little more than *Goodbye, goodbye for now; stay well like a cow?* Or has she gone on to Lermontov, Tolstoi, Chekov; does she read Pasternak and Voznesyenski?

If we knew what life had to pour in the cup, two hands together could not hold it up.

Maxine Kumin '46, A.M. '48, Radcliffe Institute '61–63, is a Pulitzer Prize-winning poet whose new books, one of poems, Our Ground Time Here Will Be Brief, New and Selected Poems *(Viking/Penguin) and a collection of short stories,* Why Can't We Live Together Like Civilized Human Beings *(Viking), were published in 1982.*

The Education of an Actor

In the late 1940s, my decision to take Broadway by storm was met with remarkable indifference by the New York theater world. I found myself living in a series of increasingly dingy and decrepit apartments, and avoided giving my father my address, lest he detect how poorly my career was going. Intrepid Yankee that he was, he nevertheless managed to track me down in the fifth-floor, cold-water hovel in which I was currently existing. His eyes did a slow pan around the one-room, overgrown closet, then he raised one eyebrow quizzically and made his only comment: "Harvard?"

He was not the last to have difficulty discerning the value of a Harvard education to an actor. Even today interviewers approach my Cambridge years as an early aberration, of interest mostly for its novelty.

Yet I always believed that Harvard was for me what it has been for tens of thousands of other alumni: simply the best preparation possible for my particular career.

Not that Harvard was any hotbed of dramatic activity in those years. Unlike today's cornucopia of theater courses, the only alternatives available for actors then were extracurricular activities, primarily the Hasty Pudding and the Dramatic Club. I still relish my memories of each of these clubs, but they were basically not professional training grounds but aggregations of talented amateurs.

But if the quality of Harvard's stages was not the best, that of its classrooms and students certainly was, and therein lies the college's great value to me. Although my major was in war sciences, thanks to NROTC commitment, I sampled enough of the college's general curriculum to acquire a solid core of knowledge that has stood me in good stead ever since. Even though the specific information of those courses often had no direct relevance to my work, each of them gave me the essential sense of assurance that comes with the feeling that one has the handle on a situation, while also stirring up the desire to learn even more about what's going on.

Such a combination of confidence and striving is the quality I associate most with Harvard students. This combination could be intimidating, but was also inspiring.

Sometimes all that my classmates seemed to have in common was their brilliance, but their diversity made my Cambridge years all the more special. I know that I've never been exposed to such a spectrum of talented people as I was at Harvard. I was also lucky enough to form lasting relationships with those whose interests and careers took directions far different from my own. Later, when I needed expert advice, I had only to call on the old school ties, as I did with Dr. John Knowles when I was preparing *Tribute.*

Our friendship was typical of the Harvard-forged bonds, even though the father of another old Harvard buddy, Rick Humphrey, predicted that "neither Knowles nor Lemmon is ever going to amount to anything." Such despair about my future was pretty endemic among my professors, because at times, I spent too little time studying, fully utilizing instead whatever acting opportunities there were.

One dean who shall remain nameless, regularly called me in about my grades, which hovered somewhere between academic probation and expulsion. "Lemmon, you're never going to make it," was his monthly admonition. When at Commencement I walked past, diploma miraculously in hand, he conceded, "Well, Lemmon, you made it through here, but you're never going to amount to anything in the real world."

Fade out, fade in. Fourteen years later, I'm on a roll. I've already won one Supporting Oscar for *Mr. Roberts,* and have just picked up successive Best Actor nominations for *Some Like It Hot* and *The Apartment*. I decide it's time to save Broadway. The great Lemmon deigns to return to the stage in a play called *Face of a Hero*. It opens at the Colonial Theater in Boston to some of the worst notices ever, with reviews beginning, "Trace of a Zero." The second night I slip out of the theater rather than face the stage-door crowd, but who should be waiting in an audience seat but my old dean. He looks up, points at me, and says, "I told you so." We both laughed, then went out together for a great night on the town.

Could such things happen at Yale?

Jack Lemmon '47, the Academy Award-winning actor, was Hasty Pudding Man of the Year in 1973.

"Them" and "Us"

I was naive. I thought that you went to college, as my parents wanted me to, lived away from home for the first time, took courses, met people, miraculously became transformed into an adult, graduated, and that was that. You didn't go back because that part of your life was over. So here I am, reminiscing about Radcliffe and Harvard, having had lots of contact with them since graduation.

I entered Radcliffe in July, 1944, at a time when Radcliffe and Harvard were on a three-term-per-year system. World War II was not yet over, and my generation, therefore, was not taking tours of Europe in the summer. What better to do than start college right away. That decision turned out well: I liked the summer term. It was smaller and more intimate than the fall and winter terms — and so I ended by going through Radcliffe in three years, taking one summer off, and finishing in a burst of glory by taking five terms in a row. I also got married in the last half of my senior year and stayed in Boston.

What was Radcliffe like then? I realize now that we met men through parties at the dorms, teas at Phillips Brooks House, and classes at Harvard after our freshman year which were still taught separately at Radcliffe. I make it sound like "them" and "us," and indeed it was. Yes, we were in the same classrooms, but, no, we were not buddies; real classmates. As for the all-male teaching staff, many were still adjusting to the shattering shock of teaching an integrated class.

It was exciting, if somewhat scarey, to be there. I learned to take in information in great gulps, especially since the summer terms, although shorter in length, were the equivalent course load of the two other terms. Try reading *War and Peace* as an extra in the summer Russian literature course that I adored. Or roar through several centuries of history in Professor Karpovich's overview which made me like history for the first time. Or learn that Latin was a real language, complete with erotic poetry, not just something through which one trudged wearily behind Caesar. Or have a top scientist try to explain in simple terms the splitting of the atom the day after the atomic bomb had been dropped. And hear Koussevitsky announce in Symphony Hall, when I was in the Radcliffe Choral Society singing — what else — Beethoven's Ninth Symphony, that the war was over.

Once I'd got my degree, I was off and running in other directions. I had five sons, I was elected to the local school committee, I was a volunteer. I thought Radcliffe was a thing of the past. But once on the mailing list of colleges, you are there forever, unless you do what one friend did and tell Harvard that you died. Ten years after I graduated, I was asked to help Radcliffe raise money. Okay, I don't mind helping. Then I became a member of the Radcliffe Alumnae Board. That beat the local PTA. Then several alumnae used Radcliffe counseling resources to analyze themselves for careers, and I wound up taking the Radcliffe Publishing Procedures Course. And that led to a job for seven years as editor of the *Radcliffe Quarterly*. I should add that a great impetus toward a career was having Polly Bunting as president of Radcliffe.

As the years went on, I discovered what everyone does: that Radcliffe/Harvard was an impeccable address that opened doors. One door it opened was that of Boston College Law School which in 1969 was delighted to have me as its oldest woman student. My learning to gulp information stood me in good stead there as I could never have gone through law school any other way.

But one cannot live on law alone — or at least I couldn't — and by 1976 I'd heard about the film studies program at Carpenter Center at Harvard. I'd been looking for something totally different as an interest to complement my law practice, and this was it. I was hooked by the time I finished the first year of basic film history, and have followed ever since what is now the Harvard Film Archive program. Carpenter Center, for those who don't know, is the building LeCorbusier designed which is next to the Fogg Art Museum and houses a variety of arts including photography, sculpture, filmmaking, and film analysis.

Back in that undergraduate setting, I learned most definitely that women at Harvard say they go to Harvard, not Radcliffe. Radcliffe is something that they vaguely know stands for female values and equality and probably is a good thing. Later some of them learn more about Radcliffe when they become graduates. However, it's clear that some day the women who went to Harvard will outnumber the women who went to Radcliffe — and what then?

Meanwhile, all of us who went to Radcliffe/Harvard were forever changed by that amazing university where it is common to have 10 famous people on campus in one day, talking or demonstrating their expertise, as an extra bonus for students who will not truly appreciate the riches heaped before them until they enter the real world where such riches are fewer and harder to find.

Maryel Finney Locke '48 is a lawyer with the firm Laurence Locke & Associates, P.C., in Boston. She is married to Laurence S. Locke '39, LLB '42.

JANE BRADLEY

How to Have a Cake and Eat It, Too

Several Harvard alumni have said to me recently, "I don't understand Radcliffe: you want to have your cake and eat it, too." They are quite right! Radcliffe women have always been doubly blessed by having a two-college affiliation. The misunderstanding arises because the relationship between Radcliffe and Harvard has been changing with each college generation to keep pace with the evolving expectations of women in our society.

When I arrived in Cambridge in 1945, I was easily recognizable as a stereotyped "Cliffie." Dressed in tweed skirt, white blouse, shetland sweater, white ankle socks and loafers, I hiked several times daily from the Radcliffe Quadrangle to Harvard Yard or Harvard Square with my green book bag slung over my shoulder. The horned-rimmed glasses did not appear until my sophomore year after I had read about three quarters of the books required for three general education courses in Philosophy, Government, and American History. The symbol of Harvard for me, was the big red book, *Courses of Instruction, Faculty of Arts and Sciences.*

I had come to Radcliffe so that I could have access to that unique book and the courses listed therein. How terribly difficult it is to choose only four or five a year from the tantalizing assortment offered. I frequently opted for big lecture classes given by well-known professors. It never occurred to me to speak to a professor in class or outside: I simply worshipped them from afar. Harvard for me was like *Alice's Looking Glass.* I stepped inside for classes and then stepped outside again as I returned to Radcliffe and my real world.

However, I was having my cake and eating it, too. In addition to my Harvard education, I was enjoying the benefits of a small women's college. The Radcliffe Quadrangle was quiet and peaceful, life in the dormitories was friendly and gracious, and the other students came from a wide variety of backgrounds, geographically and socially. The women who had chosen to come to Radcliffe all were intelligent, quite independent, and concerned with the world around them.

The hours spent with my fellow students in the small dark smoking room on the fourth floor of Briggs Hall or sipping tea and eating pastries in the Window Shop may have been detrimental to my physical health, but they opened my mind and my heart to new ideas, and they gave me an understanding and appreciation of people, their problems and their dreams. All this broadened my thinking as much as the challenging lectures in Harvard Yard. I felt privileged to be at Radcliffe and I never wished that more of the distinguished world on the other side of the Looking Glass had been mine to share.

Today, I am happily involved with Radcliffe again as an active alumna. The relationship between Radcliffe and Harvard has changed so rapidly during the past decade. Alumni, alumnae and even students are understandably confused.

When I applied to Radcliffe in 1943, I did not realize that Harvard was totally responsible for my undergraduate education. The appointment of Helen Maude Cam as the Samuel Zemurray, Jr. and Doris Zemurray Stone-Radcliffe Professor in 1947 was an exciting event, but the fact that she was the only tenured woman of the faculty did not distress me.

It was nice to have a diploma signed by both President Jordan of Radcliffe and President [James Bryant] Conant of Harvard, but

I never asked why. Today's students, however, are very aware that Radcliffe is a separate institution with its own governing board and administration. They want to know whether recent changes will help them meet the challenges they face today as women were helped in the past. Most students do not realize that Matina Horner is the first President of Radcliffe to sit on the Council of Deans and on the Faculty Council, helping to insure that the total educational experience is as good for women as for men.

Nor are most of them familiar with the Arthur and Elizabeth Schlesinger Library on the History of Women in America which is the largest, best-known research library in its field; or the Mary Ingraham Bunting Institute of Radcliffe College, which provides approximately 30 gifted women scholars and creative artists with the space, time, and financial support to pursue their work full time for one or two years; or the Henry A. Murray Research Center of Radcliffe College: A Center for the Study of Lives, which is a national repository for social science data on the changing life experience of American women; or the Radcliffe Seminars program which offers more than 100 limited-enrollment seminars to more than 1,000 part-time students ranging in age from 19 to 90. These programs have an impact on the education, careers, and quality of life of women not only at Radcliffe, but everywhere.

Radcliffe students today feel that they have genuinely equal access to all that was on the other side of my Looking Glass: libraries, athletic facilities, academic awards, and Harvard Houses. There are more tenured women on the faculty (three of whom did their research at the Bunting Institute at Radcliffe). The students benefit from their friendships with both men and women. They are doubly blessed.

A recent dinner partner of mine, an alumnus of the Harvard Class of 1945 whom I had never met before, said that he was an enlightened man and he would ask me what I was doing rather than what my husband was doing. We began talking about Radcliffe.

"One always jokes about the Cliffies but I have been impressed with the Radcliffe women I have known. I don't really understand Radcliffe, but the name is highly respected. A brilliant woman recently told me that she was able to pursue her post-doctoral work at Radcliffe when she couldn't do it anywhere else. I hope Radcliffe will hang in there!"

Radcliffe will hang in there, and I hope that Radcliffe women will continue to have their cake and eat it, too.

Jane Bradley '49, (Mrs. John M.) a recent President of the Radcliffe College Alumnae Association, serves on the Harvard Board of Overseers.

DAVID ALOIAN

Father and Son

What does a father who well remembers his own freshman year at Harvard in the 1940s think about as he watches a son get ready for his freshman year at Harvard in the 1980s? Do the experiences have something in common, or must he simply marvel at the vast chasms that separate the lives of fathers and sons?

I first saw the Yard from the steps of Lehman Hall where I had come to pick up my keys, my bursar's card, and to write out my first check to Harvard. My son first saw the Yard at my Twenty-Fifth Reunion, standing before *the* statue in his Bermuda shorts, Harvard T-shirt, his white sneakers unlaced, and his still small hand clutching the thread that held his crimson balloon.

Certainly Cambridge was different in the '40s. Ages and ages ago when I was a freshman, and it seemed to snow endlessly in Cambridge, there was not the grey eminence of Holyoke Center to loom over the Square; there were only those musty 19th-century red brick walk-ups comfortably settling into the advanced stages of genteel blight. The great slate roofs of the Memorial Hall tower, alas no longer with us, stood a head taller than all Harvard buildings.

Because Harvard Yard was a military encampment then, with V-12 Naval cadets, soon to be demobilized, billeted under the lofty elms, we entering freshmen moved directly into the River Houses. Gasoline rationing was ending, but the new postwar automobiles had not yet rolled off the assembly lines so that parking was easy. Streetcars clanged over the tracks on Massachusetts Avenue, carrying suface travellers east and west.

For us who entered Harvard in 1945, it was the dawning of the

American Age, which was to end by the time we were graduated.
It was possible then to believe that the new and shiny UN gave
assurance of eternal world peace. All that was ages and ages ago,
before computers and jets; before the cold war, Korea, Vietnam;
before plastics, TV, hi-fi's and frozen orange juice; before *Brown
vs. Topeka*, Martin Luther King and Selma; before the postwar boom
that gave us the affluent society. The tuition at Harvard College
then was $400; a good dinner at the Wursthaus cost 85 cents; gas
was 14 cents a gallon, and we paid 25 cents to see the latest films
starring Gable, Bogart or Astaire and Rogers.

Then the Square boasted of attractions such as Cronin's, Hayes
Bickford, the Oxford Grill, and Elsie's. Only Elsie's remains. The
others are gone, replaced by countless storefronts dispensing ice
cream, pizza, and croissants.

My parents stubbornly opposed my going to Harvard, fearing
that I would never come back; *his* parents have wanted Harvard for
him since his birth. I arrived by train with coal dust in my nostrils,
and two pressed-paper suitcases, after a sleepless, overnight trip
from western New York State; he arrived from the western suburbs
in a station wagon fully freighted with books, records, a hi-fi,
pictures, plants, furniture, a rug, and a few clothes. (Where will it
all fit?)

I carried ties, coats, and new white shirts; apparently he doesn't
need them. I came from a large public high school whose teachers
gave me an exaggerated sense of my intellectual powers; he comes
from an elite private school whose teachers did him no such
disservice. I was a starch-fed, occasional football player; he is a
muscled, dedicated oarsman.

I wanted to write like Hemingway; he, a freshman mind you,
scoffs at Hemingway as the eternal sophomore. My first night in
my Winthrop House room was also my first night away from home,
and I was often homesick; he has not been homesick since tennis

camp in 1975. I had not driven a car at the time I entered Harvard; he drives like Mario Andretti. But neither of us smokes, and we both enjoy beer.

Is it all so different then? Are the lives of fathers and sons always to be so disjointed and dissimilar? Perhaps not.

For I suspect that he will experience the same mute and baffled astonishment I did at the diversity, at the sheer, exasperating abundance of talent on every side of him, and at the sensitive, rough friendliness of his classmates. He'll grumble at the food as I did; he'll struggle with writing papers as I did. He will, I hope, indulge in those late-night arguments, orgies of sleeplessness that are the hallmark for all informed and contentious Harvard freshman.

He will, I hope, applaud with unashamed enthusiasm when he hears great lectures; listens to fine concerts, or watches a friend or roommate take on Chekov or Yale. He'll praise the *Crimson* and curse the *Crimson*, as we did 40 years ago.

Week by week, month by month, Harvard College will deepen him, sharpen him, disillusion him, toughen him, and yet somehow help him to define his own sense of self. Finally, I hope he will fall in love often — with young women, of course — but also with books, with bookstores, with ideas, with paintings, with music, with science and history, and literature, with learning as a way of life, and if all goes for him as it did for me, maybe even with Harvard itself.

After we left our son to begin his freshman year, there in his corner of Harvard Yard, my wife and I drove home. That night we sent him the following quotation from T. H. White's novel *The Once and Future King*. Merlin is speaking to the sulking Arthur: "The best thing for being sad is to learn something. That is the only thing that never fails. You may grow old and trembling in your anatomies, you may lie awake at night listening to the disorder of your veins, you may miss your only love, you may see the world about you devastated by evil lunatics, or know your honour trampled in the sewers of baser minds. There is only one thing for it then — to learn. Learn why the world wags and what wags it. That is the only thing which the mind can never exhaust, never alienate, never be tortured by, never fear or distrust, and never dream of regretting. Learning is the thing for you. Look at what a lot of things there are to learn."

Author of three books on the teaching of literature, David Aloian '49 is Executive Director of the Harvard Alumni Association, Master of Quincy House, and President of the Harvard Club of Boston.

ROBERT COLES

Truths that Can Last a Lifetime

For me to talk about Harvard is to talk about my whole adult life.
I came to the College after the Second World War was over. Yet
another teenager trying to grow up, get an education, and, not
least, figure out what to do with the long stretch of years ahead.

There were, at the time, a lot of older men at Harvard; they had
fought the Japanese on obscure Pacific islands, or the Germans in
various parts of Europe, and were in Cambridge to pick up the
pieces of their lives, to find one or another personal and occupa-
tional destination. I came to know several of those war veterans
quite well because we shared a tutorial with Perry Miller, a Harvard
professor who meant more to me than, even now, I know how to
say. Miller wanted us to read and understand his beloved Puritan
divines, the inspired moralists and fierce scolds, all God-obsessed
and many tormented, who lived in 18th-century New England.
He also pressed upon us Soren Kierkegaard, a strange 19th-century
Danish religious philosopher whose startling, fiery, occasionally
reckless, always penetrating essays were just becoming translated
into English. And we were asked to read Hawthorne and Melville,
neither of them in the tradition of easy, pietistic reassurance.

We sat and had our discussions; we comtemplated, at Miller's
insistence, not only theological subjects, but our own important
life experiences, or in my case, the lack thereof. I heard men speak
of blood and death on the shores of Guadalcanal. I heard men speak
of liberating the Nazi death camps — the sights and sounds of
those crematoria. Conrad's "heart of darkness" had descended upon
a so-called civilized continent, and these men, now students, saw
the result — and had a few lessons to teach their fellow students,

us callow youths who knew only the unbounded hopefulness of our naive lives.

By the time I graduated from Harvard, I was a captive of sorts. I couldn't get Perry Miller's combination of literary sensibility and historical perspective out of my head; nor could I forget the way those former soldiers and sailors connected the high-minded abstractions of intellectual life to the concrete particulars of their everyday experiences. Every time I had tried to come up with an unqualified vision, a schematic (in George Eliot's favored word, a "theoretic") notion of what ought to be, I heard Miller and those young former warriors reminding each other what had been done in this century, often enough, in the name of "science" and "progress" and "historical inevitability". Every time I was tempted to spin a web of messianic fantasies (scientific meliorism, the utopianism of applied social science, the rhetoric of one or another political agenda), I heard the voices of that tutorial, and two others I was lucky to enjoy with Perry Miller.

Harvard made life a good deal more complicated for me. There have been times when I wished that weren't the case, but I don't think many of Miller's students have wanted, in a clutch, to turn their backs on his terribly taut sense of things — that mix of idealism and brooding practicality he insisted upon presenting.

Later, while still at Harvard (as a psychiatric resident at one of its Medical School teaching hospitals, the Massachusetts General), I would have ample occasion to remember those undergraduate lessons. Probably the last major polio epidemic struck Boston in 1955; we had iron lungs all over the place, and I saw firsthand what those words "fate" and "destiny" and "luck" could come to mean in one life, then another. And still later, when I became involved as an observer in the civil rights movement, and worked as a physician with a variety of children caught up in all sorts of grim or unpromising circumstances, I kept remembering those books Miller had assigned, and most of all, the wonderfully spirited discussions he prompted — his demeanor an uncanny blend of the combative and the considerate. Moreover, my wife, who went to Radcliffe (speaking of what Harvard has meant to me!), majored in history and met up with a good number of sparks generated by Miller — the ideas of his loyal graduate students, all of them in ways marked men because his teaching grabbed hold and wouldn't let go. In home after home "down South" or "up" those Appalachian hollows, or out West, we both remembered him, remembered his doctoral students — remembered favored moments in Harvard Hall or in his Widener study, or in one or another House common room, when we were told things loud and clear and without compormise; in sum, the strangeness of this life, and the obligation one has to render human actuality as faithfully as possible.

Now that I'm back at Harvard teaching, after many years of working in that so-called "field" which social scientists speak of, I feel the example of Perry Miller every day in my head, in my bones, and I pray, in my heart. I hope to follow his lead. I worry that I fail to do so. I feel lucky to have the chance to try — and luckier, still, to have had the chance to learn, at Harvard, what is worth holding up high, as an example.

Robert Coles, MD is Professor of Psychiatry and Medical Humanities at the Harvard Medical School and Research Psychiatrist for the University Health Services. He has published more than 30 books and has won the Pulitzer Prize for Children of Crisis.

Above Everything, The Crimson

Reflection on times past tends toward optimism. Not, one suspects, because the past really was happier than today, but because, however acutely we felt its discomforts while they were occurring, we did in fact live through them. The chief attraction of personal history is that one has survived. Yet my recollections of Harvard College, gilded though they are, seem floating in anxiety, like a movie projected onto a wall of smoke.

My Harvard-driven *angst* began a whole year before my first registration. In that Jurassic era, one did not receive Early Decisions, or even Seasonable Decisions: the sweating and vibrating lasted until the end, which for the Class of 1953 did not come until June 10, 1949. I had actually received my high school diploma before I learned of my chance to receive one from Harvard.

Anxiety continued after arrival. The place was so big; the work so intensive; the familiar cocoon of my old school so distant. Yet even in the misery, a glimmer of joy shone through. I remember crossing the Yard one gray November afternoon and comforting myself by thinking that even if I were miserable, I would rather be unhappy at Harvard than at any place on earth.

When Christmas vacation ended, however, the orientation had changed. Entering the Yard, I felt that I was returning to my own place; for the next three and a half years, the feeling repeated itself every time I came back after an absence.

The anxiety lingered on, though. It took various forms, focusing on different episodes: academic impedimenta, papers, and exams; House acceptance; the start of the Korean War; enlistment into the Naval Reserve; acceptance into an esoteric Navy officer candidate program; a series of Radcliffe connections (and disconnections); law school applications; a thesis.

But above everything, the *Crimson*.

Of all the Harvard organizations, no other — not even any of the theater groups — quite attained the Crime's professionalism. Beyond that, the *Crimson* viewed the real world (as opposed to the Harvard world) in a uniquely cirtical way. It was not that the Crimeds were the only Harvard students to believe sincerely that national (or international) affairs needed improvement. A whole gamut of political cadres, from the John Reed Club to the Harvard Young Republicans, joyously let fly at the current Establishment. The *Crimson*, however, seemed then, and in retrospect seems now, to have been the only group not just talking, but doing.

The twin themes of professionalism and direct involvement burned themselves into the souls of everyone who was able to qualify for the *Crimson's* frankly elitist cohort. Thus, in 1949–50 the newly elected editors (all *Crimson* members were "editors," the way all policemen are "officers") included such future titans of disciplined excellence and commitment as Daniel Ellsberg, Michael J. Halberstam, and G. Jerome W. Goodman (better known nowadays as Adam Smith).

From the moment a prospective candidate walked into the glaringly grubby newsroom, he was made to realize that the *Crimson*, although willing to examine his abilities fairly, officially doubted their sufficiency. Like many an elite organization — the United States Marine Corps comes to mind — the *Crimson* openly expressed and frequently repeated the presumption that a candidate could not meet its standard of acceptance.

The *Crimson's* equivalent of boot camp was called a competition. For almost three months, candidates competed, not against each other, but against their initial inability to make the *Crimson's* grade. Each had to acquire, at top speed, an arsenal of new skills: quick accurate, readable writing; precise copy measuring; following orders; showing initiative in obtaining "originals," stories the paper would not have gotten but for the candidate's effort; obeying orders; taking harsh public criticism unflinchingly; anticipating orders; and devoting so much time to the enterprise that one mother, noting her son's difficulty in finding time to write home, referred to the paper as "the Criminal."

All this training did not result from self-study. The editors took a direct and often profane part in the process. Understandably, they believed in their own abilities, a belief which the facts fully warranted. The *Crimson* in those days was a redoubt of giants. Hindsight, it is true, always magnifies. Yet even in 1950, one could comfortably predict that such *Crimson* standouts as (for example) Chuck Bailey, Bill Green, Paul Mandel, and Peter Taub would not go into advertising or wholesale dry goods. (Of these, in fact, Green was the only one who did not become a first-rank journalist, but he did go on to take away Bella Abzug's Congressional seat.)

Along with their consummate journalistic skills and the editors' air of total competence went, as I have suggested, a determined and zestful plunge into the vortex of serious and significant controversy. The *Crimson* battled the NROTC over loyalty oaths; and at the height of Senator McCarthy's power it annually surveyed the condition of academic freedom, nation-wide, a service that no other newspaper dared to attempt. The *Crimson* got angry about things that counted; the *Crimson* tried, in a direct way, to make them better. Paul Mandel's Ed One on the 1952 Pogo Riot is unequalled, even today, as an essay on police overreaction.

The nature of what the *Crimson* was, and did, meant that working for it kept one in a state of anxious tension. The pressure never let up: the Crime even published thrice weekly during examination period.

Yet although Justice Holmes once remarked that anxiety is what kills, the *Crimson*, more than any other College experience, gave shape to my life, my outlook, my attitudes, my expectations of myself and others, and my professional standards. I suppose I would have come to manhood without the Crime. But I am quite certain I would have turned out tamer and duller. The *Crimson's* tension was like a spring being coiled; it has constantly impelled me ever since.

Hiller B. Zobel '53, LLB '59, wrote The Boston Massacre *and is an Associate Justice of the Massachusetts Superior Court.*

THE PUSEY YEARS

1953 — 1971

EDWARD M. HOAGLAND

A Palace in a Yard

I loved living in such a majestic place as Harvard Yard — I never will again! It was like being a year-long guest in the palace outbuildings of a benign but ever-distant king. Though not a democratic setting, for us freshmen it soon became a city in itself, with fellow scholars who gave illegal haircuts for 50¢, sold dry goods, or maintained dissolute dives. One could go next door and hear Archibald MacLeish lecture on the poetry of Li Po, or to Phillips Brooks house, next door on the other side, where Howard Fast, "broken"-looking, shaking, wearing a prison pallor (this was the McCarthy era), talked about his recent spell in jail.

Widener Library awed me when I lived in front of it during that freshman year. But when I had the run of the library as an upperclassman, I joyfully wrote a novel on the "C" basement level there. Deep, deep down, three basements under those millions of volumes, I felt bolstered by the company — somehow all the freer about composing my own.

Not only Widener Library but the Harvard of the Houses was one of the world's few democracies. We could do anything as juniors and seniors — read Shakespeare's 36 plays, roam Boston day and night, pour out our hearts to friends the way an "adult" seldom will. And Boston was my first real city — my Paris and Hong Kong. I haunted Revere Beach, and worked in the circus when it came to town; yet had five, first-class writer-mentors at college to show my chapters to. The friends one finds at such an extraordinary university, and the faculty people one intently studies and casually listens to, represent a spread of personalities that remain as a point of reference always afterwards.

Edward M. Hoagland '54, has written Red Wolves and Black Bears, Walking the Dead Diamond River, The Courage of Turtles, Notes from the Century Before, The Peacock's Tail, The Circle Home, Cat Man, *and a travel book about the Sudan.*

JOHN UPDIKE

Taking Courses

I had a lot to learn when I came to Harvard, which was fortunate, since Harvard had a lot to teach. College reminiscences tend to focus on friendship and foolery and the anxious bliss of being young; and there was that for me, too. But I loved, strange to say, taking courses — the pre-semester shopping in the crimson-bound catalogue, its aisles bulging with goodies from *Applied Mechanics* to *Zoology*, and then the concoction of the schedule, with due avoidance of any class meeting before 10, and then the attendance, the sedate amusement of going to an antiquated lecture hall, its every desk pitted with the initials of the departed, and being entertained for an hour with a stream of things one hadn't known before.

Of the 32 half-courses that made up my requisite 16 credits, every one was a more or less delightful revelation, beginning with the person of the instructor. These men (not one class I took, it just now occurs to me, was taught by a woman) seemed heroic to the point of comedy, having devoted their lives to erudition. *Math 1a and 1b (Introduction to Calculus*, under a straw-haired section man whose name I have forgotten but whose innocently proud way of swooping an inscrutable equation onto the blackboard I still can picture) cured me of my freshman notions of being a math major; I turned to English, and concentrated earnestly.

Francis Magoun, raptly chanting the gutteral language of his cherished Anglo-Saxons, his arms jutting out in imitation of clashing broadswords; Hyder Rollins, erect and white-haired, with a beautifully unreconstructed Southern accent, calmly reducing the romanticism of Byron, Keats, and Shelley to a matter of variorum editions; Walter Jackson Bate, bringing the noble agony of Sam

Johnson to startling life at the lectern; Douglas Bush, with his bald, bowed head and squeezed voice and amiable dry wit, leading us doggedly through the petrified forests of Spenser and Milton; Kenneth Murdoch, folding his arms just like Jack Benny and allowing with a sigh that the metaphysicals could be tedious — these were some of the giants of the department in those days. Of these only Harry Levin, who taught a course in Joyce, Proust, and Mann as well as one on Shakespeare, offered any sense of access to the world of modern, living letters — it was common undergraduate knowledge that he had written the sole contemporary review of *Finnegans Wake* that Joyce had much liked. His lectures on Shakespeare, delivered with a slightly tremulous elegance to a huge throng in Emerson, not only opened my eyes to our supreme classic but, with their emphasis on dominant metaphor, to a whole new way of reading. Some of the smaller courses were among the best — Edwin Honig's quizzical, soft-spoken survey of the modern poets; Robert Chapman's bouncy seminar in George Bernard Shaw; Kenneth Kempton's resolutely professional writing course, in which he read aloud to us those magical early stories by Salinger.

The early '50s are now considered a politically torpid era, but we did have our excitements that stirred reactions even within our heavy scholastic cocoon — Joe McCarthy (against), Adlai Stevenson (for), the Checkers speech (against), the Korean War (for, as long as somebody else was fighting it). My most vivid national memory is of holding up a pencil, in short-lived Allston Burr Hall, to signify my readiness to take a simple-minded test that would prove my fitness to be temporarily exempt from the draft. Nobody at the time, to my knowledge, questioned the justice of these procedures, or declined their deferment. It was a dog-eat-dog world, of doing your own thing before it was called that.

It was, for many, an intensely literary time — how we worshipped, and gossiped about, Eliot and Pound and those other textual archangels! Eliot and Frost, Cummings and Stevens, Dylan

Thomas and Carl Sandburg all made appearances at Harvard in those four years, and Thornton Wilder and Vladimir Nabokov taught courses. Literature was in. Pop music was Patti Paige and Perry Como, the movies were Doris Day and John Wayne, and youth culture was something that happened, if anywhere, at summer camp.

We wore gray coats and narrow little neckties, like apprentice deacons, or would-be section men. Some English majors did in fact become section men and PhDs and professors, promulgating the great texts to yet younger generations. To me that seemed a frightening prospect; my capacity for other people's words was limited. I peaked, as a scholar, in my junior year and capped my academic career with a dull thesis and a babbling display of ignorance at my oral examination. Four years was enough Harvard. I still had a lot to learn, but had been given the liberating notion that now I could teach myself.

John Updike '54 is the author of 20-odd books of which the most recent is a novel, The Witches of Eastwick.

Green Years at the Crimson

The memory is very clear, and it stands as if fixed in time. It is February 1954, I am 19 years old and the managing editor of a daily newspaper. It is only a college daily, but my colleagues and I go about it as if we are editing *The New York Times*, which secretly (and indeed not so secretly) most of us eventually intend to do. A group of us are sitting around *The Crimson* newsroom at 2:30 in the morning. The pressrun is about to start. This is the first issue of our editorial board, and we are inordinately proud of what we have produced.

Tony Lukas, who is our best reporter and has covered Joseph McCarthy from the start (he has McCarthy's private number, and we love to listen in, thrilling as McCarthy calls Lukas by his first name), has scored a journalistic coup. For more than a year he has reported on the trials and charges against Wendell Furry, a relatively obscure Harvard professor of physics. (Thirty years later I can still remember Furry's middle name, since McCarthy liked using middle names as if he were reading from a police blotter: Wendell *Hinckle* Furry.) Lukas has gotten to know Furry quite well, mentioning to him in the process that if he ever wanted to talk about his past, Lukas would be delighted to report it. Finally, Furry has said yes, and in this issue Lukas has a long and brilliant piece of why Furry joined the Communist party, what it was like and why he got out. Our pride in Lukas's accomplishment is immense; it sheds light where most people have been shedding darkness. Afterward it runs unedited on the Associated Press wire, and the managing editor of the *St. Louis Post-Dispatch* immediately calls to offer Lukas a job.

Lukas protests that he is only a junior in college. "Then come for the summer," says the editor.

This does not surprise us, for Lukas, though he is our own age, is something of a role model. He and I started out in the same freshman competition two years earlier, and it had been staggering to me to see how finished he was, not just as a reporter but as someone who had already thought about the ethics of being a reporter. He was then 18 years old. He came from a home where people argued politics, and he already had a complete and defined value system that he could readily bring to journalism. He was broodingly serious and thoughtful; what we were doing on *The Crimson* was in no way parochial, it was in the most immediate and profound sense connected to issues in the real world. That someone as intelligent and worldly as Tony Lukas wanted to be a reporter and thought it a profession worthy of his talent is encouraging, for he is on his way to a magna cum laude in government, and some of the best professors at Harvard are arguing with him to become an academic.

Sitting in *The Crimson* newsroom that night were Jack Langguth, the president, Dick Ullman, the editorial chairman, Lukas and I. We had been, in months just past, at once the closest of friends and the fiercest of competitors, bonded by our loyalty to this strange little institution and at the same time with the relationships among us sharpened by the exhausting competition for the jobs we now held. That night Langguth went over to the comment book, where the ongoing marathon debate on style, taste, quality and ethics took place, and wrote in a small, neat hand: "Not a bad first issue, JAL II." JAL II is Lukas — Jay Anthony Lukas — and since we go by initials, the number two is to distinguish him from Joseph Anthony Lewis, managing editor in 1947, who had gone on to work on a small daily in Washington. Then we went off to the Hayes Bick for a late meal, taking with us a copy of the paper so we could argue until 4:00 A.M. How we will make our morning classes no one knows; classes seem very distant from us on an occasion as extraordinary as this. Looking back on those years, when our generation was considered completely quiescent, I am awed by our degree of political involvement.

David Halberstam '55 won a Pulitzer Prize in 1964 for his reporting from New York. His books include The Best and the Brightest *and* The Powers That Be.

ROBERT D. STOREY

A Myth Dispelled

Harvard is not a college, it is a state of mind. It is a *WELTAN-SCHAUUNG*, confirmed or acquired in Cambridge, which Harvard people, like Englishmen under the Empire, carry with them wherever they go. This can be a problem for non-Harvard others, who sometimes view Harvardians (like the aforementioned Englishmen) as a bit insufferable. Harvard people call it "indifferent."

When pressed on the subject, Harvard graduates will concede that it is Harvard's style to keep such qualities as warmth, spontaneity, enthusiasm, and flexibility under control. But Harvard has, in Churchill's phrase, a soft underbelly. I know this to be true, as evidenced by what follows.

I wasn't going to Harvard. After four years at Exeter, I decided in March of my senior year to return to the unpretentious Midwest and to leave the affectation and pseudo-sophistication of the East behind me. Accordingly, I wrote to the Admissions Office at Harvard and requested that my name be withdrawn from the list of applicants for the Class of 1958. I would attend Oberlin.

A funny thing happened on my way back to Ohio. During the summer of 1954, I did volunteer work in the East End of London with seven Exeter classmates, five of whom were going to Harvard. Though they made no conscious effort to do so, they gradually influenced me to reconsider my college plans. I began to realize that the East had really become a part of me. I was in fact more at ease in New England and with Easterners than I had previously been willing to admit. Unfortunately, this important bit of self-awareness did not become clear to me until August of 1954, long after Harvard had determined the composition of its freshman class!

Nonetheless, my friends — already manifesting that mix of assurance and audacity which Harvardians seem destined to possess in uncommon abundance — encouraged me to make an 11th-hour effort to gain admission to the College. Thus prompted, I wrote to Exeter's Principal, William G. Saltonstall (Harvard '28) from Paris and confessed my sin: I had grievously erred and I now really wanted to go to Harvard. Salty graciously wrote back that what I had in mind was a bit unorthodox, but that he would discuss the matter with William Bender, Harvard's incomparable Dean of Admissions.

Around August 15th, I again heard from Salty who suggested that I stop by Harvard upon my return to the United States and chat with Dean Bender. On a Saturday morning during the second week of September, I arrived in Cambridge and rushed to Dean Bender's office. He was raking leaves at his home, having left word at his office that he be informed of my arrival. As I sat waiting anxiously for the Dean, Byron Stookey, one of his assistants, saw me and asked, "Are you Storey?" I answered yes. He then said, "Have you gotten room yet?" I thought he meant a room for the weekend, while Harvard decided my fate. It wasn't until Dean Bender arrived — taking a break from his leaf-raking — that I learned I had indeed been admitted to Harvard, effective immediately. Being a dutiful son, I thereupon called my parents to inform them that I would not be coming home until Christmas. I informed Oberlin that I would not be coming there at all.

Dean Bender told me that the Admission Committee was able to take this most extraordinary action on my behalf only because my file had been reviewed in depth earlier. Also, that the Committee members appreciated that I had shown the courtesy of timely advising them that I did not plan to attend Harvard. He also suggested I not discuss the matter further.

A Myth Dispelled

Thus, for the friendly encouragement of certain members of the Class of 1958, the good offices of Bill Saltonstall, and the sympathetic understanding of Bill Bender, I never would have had the privilege of taking courses taught by such professors as Crane Brinton, Karl Friedrich, Frederick Merk, Perry Miller, Paul Tillich, McGeorge Bundy, Ernest May, Henry Kissinger, Zbigniew Brzezinski, and Benjamin Schwartz. Nor would I have enjoyed Harvard-Yale weekends, Bogart Festivals at the Brattle Theatre, Red Sox-Yankee games at Fenway Park, visits to the Cape with my roommates, special dinners at Locke-Ober's, or evenings of sherry and pleasant conversation with John Conway, Master of Leverett House. Nor, most important, would I have met my wife, a member of the Radcliffe Class of 1959.

Because of Bill Saltonstall, Bill Bender, and others, I learned that Harvard is not hopelessly indifferent. Now, nearly 30 years later, I am — with suitably restrained enthusiasm, I trust — happy to confirm it.

Robert David Storey '58, partner in the Cleveland law firm of Burke, Haber & Berick, was Chief Marshal for the 1983 Commencement Exercises. He is a member of the Cleveland City Planning Commission and has been a Harvard Overseer.

The Ordeal of Going to Harvard

Perhaps it was preordained that I'd go to Harvard. My father, his father before him, my mother's brother, and her father, a slew of my cousins, as well as two godfathers and a whole circle of my parents' friends — they had all gone to Harvard.

But then, in 1949, my father suddenly moved us West and bought a ranch outside the then-near-ghost town of Aspen, Colorado. After a couple of years it seemed that the Eastern ties had been broken.

The year before we left New York, my father had taken me up to see Groton. It had scared me to death. It was also my first political experience. The combination of seeing all those Dewey posters and being intimidated by the Groton atmosphere, had made me assume that Dewey would be our next President. Later, in Colorado, I saw Harry Truman campaigning from the back of a train. That solidified both Western and Democratic tendencies.

I first visited Harvard as a high school junior, got lost in a maze of identical-looking brick buildings, finally found my cousin Sabin, who showed me around, but I hated it and felt totally out of place.

As my senior year at Fountain Valley School rolled along, none of us seemed much interested in college. So I applied to Harvard, sensing an unspoken but intense family pressure but also wondering if maybe I was too young for college, thinking that perhaps I should go into the Army or maybe even wander off to the rodeo circuit. It was Dana Cotton, who came out to Fountain Valley each year, who finally began to get me focused and to help me sense what an extraordinary opportunity Harvard could be for me.

That summer, two of my future roommates, Dana's son, John,

and Kim Kimball, Exeter graduates, came by our ranch, both fresh from a summer of working at Yellowstone Park. Even though we quickly became friends, it was tough to wrench myself away from the West. A week before school started, I went off to Rifle, Colorado for the Labor Day Rodeo, a weekend of saddle broncs, dance halls, wild horse races, Coors beer, and carnivals. When I got home, ragged, broke, my shoulder partially dislocated from getting bucked off once too often, it was time to settle down, head east, face up to Harvard. I was nervous and depressed.

The "Harvard experience" began with fits and starts. I loved the freedom of those first days, searching around Cambridge for an old refrigerator, driving up into New Hampshire, plodding through those horrible muggy afternoon football practices as a soreshouldered, near-sighted, 155-pound high school guard turned halfback. A flash of light came when an English instructor singled out a short story for special praise, then began reading it to the class. I jerked awake, realizing that it was mine. Then the painful transition from a high school hockey star to a struggling bit-player on a powerful freshman team. Later in the year, wandering through a swampy field near Concord, I realized that it was suddenly spring and the ground was alive again.

I came to love Harvard, to look forward to September, to turning my horses out to pasture, loading up the car, gathering up a few Wellesley, St. Lawrence or Harvard-bound friends and beginning that nonstop cross-country drive, back into sweltering Cambridge.

The people who sustained me? Most of all, Dana Cotton, who watched over us and nudged us along. If he could love Harvard as much as he did, then I could, I told myself, put in a little effort for the place. Richard Poirier, who woke me up as a writer when I was a junior. All the people in Winthrop House, even the master who wrote Kimball, Cotton, and me an angry note in the spring of our sophomore year, predicting that "one by one we would fade from the Harvard scene" and then got fired himself. All those other groups that I drifted in and out of — the rugby team, the Spee and Pi Eta Clubs, that pathetic little group of us who made up the "Romance Language and Literature" majors, Henry Lamont's boxers.

Perhaps most of all, I owe thanks to those pale, faceless "moles" who inhabited the cubicles around me in the depths of Lamont Library. For years we would pass each other wordlessly in the halls or stand silently shoulder to shoulder in the men's rooms, with never a word of welcome or acknowledgement. Was I invisible? Were they scared of me? Did they sense that I wasn't serious, that I was one of those guys who didn't go to classes, who sprinted through a dozen books in the last 48 hours to land clumsily on a C+. Perhaps I've realized that they too were struggling. Perhaps that's why I was so thrilled last year to be elected to the Harvard Alumni Association and to begin making those journeys eastward again.

Morgan Smith '60 is the Executive Director of the Colorado Department of Local Affairs, a director of the Harvard Alumni Association and former president of the Rocky Mountain Harvard Club.

Pretty Good for a Second Choice!

Radcliffe was not my first choice. I applied because of its reputation, but with my interest in classics, Bryn Mawr seemed at the time to have a greater appeal. Besides, my initial contacts with Radcliffe were discouraging, to say the least. My first application went astray; when I went for my local interview, the alumna representative had forgotten the appointment and gone out to the theater! I decided not to take the time to visit Cambridge.

Fortunately, some weeks later, I was invited to Groton for the weekend, and decided to spend a day at Radcliffe, since I would be passing through Boston anyway. I still have vivid memories of that visit; the warm welcome of my hostess, a dinner party off-campus with stimulating conversation, a rewarding interview at the Admissions Office; but, best of all, I was privileged to attend lectures by Walter Bate and Seymour Slive. I was absolutely overwhelmed, and became convinced that this was the college for me.

In the fall of 1956, I headed off for Cambridge, a naive freshman from a small private girls' school. The adjustment to coeducation was not easy my first year. But I survived, and after a brief flirtation with science, returned to my original love of Greek language and literature. I feel particularly fortunate to have majored in classics, a field with relatively few concentrators. My classes were small, never more than 25, and it was easier to get to know one's professors. What a privilege to study Pindar with John Finley, Homer with Cedric Whitman, Plato with Eric Havelock, Virgil with Zeph Stewart, and Thucydides with Sterling Dow!

My junior year I had the unusual opportunity to have as my tutor a visiting scholar named George Huxley, subsequently a Fellow of

All Souls at Oxford. He introduced me to the exacting standards of classical studies in England, and was shocked to learn that I had never taken a composition course. (At Harvard one could avoid the composition course by writing a senior thesis.) Despite my protests, he insisted that I try my hand at rendering English prose into Greek, and patiently helped me improve my initial stumbling efforts. Since I eventually became a Byzantinist, and have spent many years trying to master medieval Greek, I am grateful for this excellent training in the classical form of the language.

It was not only my classics courses that made a lasting impression on me. When I reminisce now about my college experience, I find that in many cases I remember the professors better than the subject matter they taught. Almost 25 years after graduation I have forgotten all the formulas I memorized in *Chem I*, but have vivid recollections of Eugene Rochow's dramatic demonstrations, for example, of a large tooth dissolving in a vat of Coca-Cola! Neither do I remember the explanation of the Doppler effect; but I will never forget the excitement of Allen Hynek's lectures, and the drama of his announcement of the launching of Sputnik.

One of the happy coincidences of my experience at Harvard-Radcliffe was the way in which I was able to combine extracurricular activities with my academic interests. In Cambridge I was introduced to the pleasures of amateur theater production, and was involved in numerous plays produced by the Harvard Dramatic Club and House dramatic societies. Those were the days before the Loeb and the renovation of Agassiz, when one had to cope with lack of fly space, inadequate wings, workshops, and dressing rooms. The lightboards were antique, threatening to electrocute the operator. But we learned to improvise, presented a number of memorable plays, and made lasting friendships. Most important for me, backstage at Eliot House, in the kitchen, I met my future husband the night we struck *Titus Andronicus*.

I always worked backstage, except for the time I was persuaded to play the corpse in *Revenger's Tragedy.* I loved building sets, finding props, and the excitement of the live performance. I also became interested in the production of ancient Greek plays, and the architecture of the theaters. So it was inevitable that I should end up producing the Classical Society's performance of the *Clouds,* in the original Greek, in the courtyard of the Fogg Museum. A somewhat unconventional setting perhaps for Aristophanes, but quite effective. Unfortunately our plan to lower Socrates from the balcony in a bosun's chair fell through because we could not rent one at the dockyards, and we had to improvise with lights.

I wrote my thesis on satyr plays, and included a chapter on theater production in ancient Greece. To me Harvard represented a land of wondrous opportunity, where one could pursue almost any interest, and find other students or faculty members who shared similar enthusiasms.

I consider my four years in Cambridge among the happiest of my life. I am grateful for the exhilaration of the classroom, the excitement of the theater, and the many friends with whom I still feel a special kinship, even though we are scattered and do not see each other very often.

When I look back now, however, upon my education at Radcliffe and Harvard in the Eisenhower-Pusey era, I perceive two serious problems, which the college has gone far to rectify during the past 15 years. First of all, my generation of Radcliffe students was deprived of the experience of living in a Harvard House; in the late '50s we Cliffies, living in the Annex, had a vague sense of being "second-class citizens," but accepted the situation without protest. Even more shocking to me now is the realization that in four years I was exposed to only one woman professor, the redoubtable astronomer Cecilia Payne-Gaposchkin. It never occurred to me at the time that anything was amiss with a system in which women students had only male teachers.

I am thankful that times have changed, that co-residential living has been instituted, and the number of women professors is slowly increasing. Harvard-Radcliffe offered extraordinary educational opportunities in the 1950s; I am sure that now the experience is even better, especially for women.

Alice-Mary Maffry Talbot '60 is Executive Editor of the Dictionary of Byzantium, currently in preparation, and First Vice President of the HAA. She is married to William S. Talbot '59.

A "Mother" and a Fond One

I owe to Harvard sanity.

A trembling 17-year-old, I rushed into the Admissions office to protest my "yellow passport," a mimeographed form accepting me as a freshman if I would agree to live at home (which meant for me confinement to the Jewish streets of Dorchester and Mattapan). I was a low B student, a victim of the rituals of rote memory at the Boston Public Latin School. Harvard perhaps has an exaggerated beauty for me in reaction to what I perceived as four years in a "blacking factory" out of Dickens.

Looking back now on high school, I realize that I did acquire a valuable stock of English verse there, and the will to compete, but the price was too great. I was angry, paranoid, tore at my face, and went about feeling like Raskolnikoff on the eve of his crime. Colleges like great vines have special years — 1957-61 showed a special vintage, perhaps the last years in which from parochial New England, hundreds of boys from Boston and the Massachusetts towns would be mingled with wider cultures of the world, the best students of California, Hawaii, English royalty, and Arab princes.

I was asked what *I* thought. This was what the '50s called an "existential" shock. Not in all courses, for a freshman had to grind through the usual information tallies but even in a dull stretch like *Natural Science*, the instructor was willing to overlook poor mathematics for the sake of Alfred North Whitehead and my clumsy pondering over the aim of science.

The college, Harvard, of that era, trusted its students; admitted, it was assumed that you were competent. Specific accounting could be postponed, the first task was to *think*. This accorded to all of us callow freshmen a certain dignity which it is impossible to over-estimate.

I came to live on the campus during the second half of my freshman year and the mystique of the Yard, its atmosphere of monastic seclusion even through the high jinks, hallowed the long nights of reading and the tasks of mid-terms and finals. I was brash, loud, noisy, and had an immediate success in the Harvard theatrical productions.

But what I recall now is Reuben Brower's *Humanities 6*, a course which quietly set me off in new directions. The first term I had an indifferent section instructor and Professor Brower's voice was so low and gentle that one had difficulty hearing it beyond the first 20 rows. An inveterate latecomer, I lost much of what was said in lectures, but my section instructor the second term was the now famous critic, Richard Poirier. For the first time I heard the voices in English literature — a revelation — Poirier's reading aloud D. H. Lawrence, making us conscious of the author's ironic intentions. A difficult term for me — Poirier spoke to me about theater in Harvard Square as if we were equals and then to my consternation handed back one of my papers with the terse notation, "You couldn't possibly have meant this. Rewrite." Insisting that we come up to the level of their own thoughts, one's instructors at Harvard conferred the Bachelor's degree upon one at the outset.

Humanities 6 was the *pons asinorum* to the Harvard which asked one in Philosophy, sociology, drama, to query first what the book or play intended on its own terms and then demand of oneself a response. In the best courses — David Riesman's, Erik Erikson's, Robert Chapman's remarkable class which humbly masqueraded as workshop in stage managing but which gave one the intellectual dimensions of the modern theater, Albert Guerard's classes in writing and lectures on the psychology of the modern novel —

one met this flattering but firm finger in one's buttonholes, "What is happening and where are *you*?"

Again, I was fortunate to have been domiciled at Kirkland House where William Alfred taught nightly in table conversation which left one dazzled, leaping from the erudite to the earthy, and where the Master, Charles Taylor, and his Senior Tutor, Bob O'Claire, acted as devoted but unpretentious parents. The House, its Christmas plays, its table talk, its formal dinners with visiting intellectuals like Aldous Huxley and actors like Jason Robards, endowed me with a sense of nobility in education, of wide horizon, of membership in the tradition of English and American culture: made me more willing to ask of myself, what is there to value in the Jewish streets of Boston and their antecedents.

Harvard was remarkable too, at this juncture, in securing as its rabbi, Ben-Zion Gold, who, despite the horrors of Auschwitz, was as eager to learn about America as he was to speak about the lost worlds of Eastern Europe. When I graduated, I felt a pride that was almost dangerous because the institution had been so gracious to me. When I met William Alfred and Ben Gold after college, I felt I was still their student and that our fellowship was lifelong. After all, it was out of a ring of ideas that one was riding and to which one would return again and again. Once in Rome, I encountered Professor Brower on the landscaped brow of the American Academy, spent a golden hour walking its grounds, talking with him, testing ideas of mine against his enthusiasm. At such moments I seem to pass in the circles of a garden out of time.

I am often angry at Harvard now, because it meant so much to me, most of all confidence in judgment, yet willingness always to think again, and it really was the best of worlds for four years. One expects inspiration and leadership throughout one's life from the institution and when, in maturity, one discovers that it is sadly human and fallible, that the college and university can not always muster the self-criticism of its best teachers, then one grows angry and short-tempered as at a parent. My father, Wilfred Mirsky '29, passed away this year and, alas, I find it difficult now to trenchantly criticize Harvard, which was to both of us what its Latin tag promised, a "mother" and a fond one.

Mark Mirsky '61 is the author of four novels and former Professor of English at The City College of New York.

I Want to Go to Yale

As my own Twenty-Fifth Reunion approaches, my mind goes back to my first trip to Harvard at age six. The occasion was father's Twenty-Fifth Reunion in 1946, right after World War II. I was not aware of the impact the war was having on Harvard, certainly not at age six. It was my first long trip away from home and Cambridge seemed like a busy, crowded, hot place in June.

Harvard was a "big thing" at home. My grandfather had gone there and so had my uncle, and my brother was beginning to think seriously about applying. My father, a loyal Harvard man, had four sons, so it was natural that he might do a little proselytizing. But at age six, Harvard was a distant and incomprehensible phenomenon.

I had been to the Harvard-Yale game in New Haven and knew that Yale was the "enemy." That day the "enemy" won but fortunately the band was good and I was too young to understand the game. My father convinced me of the inevitability of Harvard if I excelled in kindergarten and forever thereafter.

In retrospect, I confess that my parents' activities at the reunion seemed akin to my own activities in kindergarten. Once in Cambridge, it became obvious that I would not be a major part of their Twenty-Fifth. My parents would spend little time with me and I would be inundated with seven- and eight-year-olds in children's activities and games. Some 15 years later as an undergraduate reunion worker myself, I realized what poison I must have been.

At six I was just about as young a child as reunion officials would allow to attend. From my perspective, in addition to being away from me all the time, my parents seemed to be in a highly congenial mood that was unfamiliar. There were friends of my father — people whom I had heard him talk about and to whom I was introduced at the beginning: Mr. and Mrs. Nichols, Mr. and Mrs. Larsen, Mr. and Mrs. Godfrey, Mr. and Mrs. Lamont, Mr. Mc-Cord, and so on. It looked like great fun . . . for mom and dad. Their reunion friends wore lime-green-and-white striped neckties with 21, 21, 21 everywhere. The ladies wore, or more often carried, lime green-and-white hats. They looked silly to me and the ladies of 21 must have felt similarly because there were more carriers than wearers of the hats.

Father, mother, my 15-yeard-old brother, and I were staying in Kirkland House. It seemed dark and small after our large, airy house at home. The walls had picture hooks, but no pictures. There were dark desks, chairs and beds in the room, but little else. Worst of all, there was only one bathroom. At home we had three. Harvard did not live up to my father's advanced billing. From my point of view, our stay at Harvard could not have been too short. I was miserable.

Meanwhile, my brother was having a fine time. Touch football, softball, dances, and movies kept him on the go. Girls surrounded him and I even think he had a sip of beer. He spent less time with me than my parents.

I felt adrift. Herded with other munchkins from place to place by well-meaning Radcliffe girls (how I would have relished that attention 12 to 14 years later), I was miserable. I even cried.

Bitterly I was led with my group across the river to what I now realize was the Business School. We played the obligatory games of kick-the-can or softball and then lined up for lunch. Children's food at the Twenty-Fifth was mostly good, especially the desserts. We almost always had ice cream, and plenty of it. Such was not the case; hot dogs and cabbage broke the dam. Ignored by my parents, forced to play kick-the-can, and finally, hot dogs and cabbage instead of hamburgers and ice cream. I blurted out, "I want to go to *Yale.*" I planned that when my parents came back from their endless round of clambakes, softball games, beach parties, museum tours, dances, and cocktails, I would repeat it to them 100 times at the top of my lungs if need be, "I want to go to *Yale.*"

What was the reaction of the kind reunion volunteers as my eyes filled with tears? Where were my parents? Why was my brother having so much fun? Most important, had everyone forgotten about me in all this *Harvard* reunion confusion?

At last, my father and mother returned. The "sixes, sevens, and eights" were driven back to Kirkland House and I thought better of repeating my insult. But a treacherous reunion aide told my father. He thought it amusing; mother smiled.

Apparently the remark spread like wildfire through the reunion. Father's friends and even strangers came by for a look. "So you're the young man thinking of Yale," said far too many 21ers. Embarrassed and disgraced at the age of six; Harvard was certainly out of the picture for me, I concluded, as were my father's fondest hopes. My brother intimated that the aftermath might even be worse than that.

Driving home, my parents convinced me that the blasphemous remark was more humorous than insulting. All was forgotten.

Harvard also survived the insult and Twenty-Fifth Reunions are still being held. Nor did Harvard hold any grudges. I was admitted to the Class of 1961 on April 15, 1957. Happily for me, I never followed up on my threat of almost 40 summers ago. I have noticed, however, that six-year-olds are no longer invited to their father's Twenty-Fifth. I hope it was not because of my insult.

A. Bronson Thayer '62 is President of the Harvard Alumni Association. He is Vice President, Finance, Lykes Bros. Inc., in Tampa, Florida, and Chairman of First Florida Banks.

The Many Faces of Harvard

My elder brother was a junior when I entered Harvard; we drove
north to Cambridge together. He pointed out with lordly lack of
interest those stages of the journey I was gawking at. He had the
perfect condescension of the initiate; he dropped names with such
assurance I was certain we'd be welcomed by the President himself.
In Watertown we waited for pedestrians. Twenty people crossed
the street; my brother indicated one. "There," he said. "that fellow
there. The one with the gray herringbone. That's a Cambridge
face."

I asked him how he knew. He was, I think, saved by the light;
he busied himself shifting gears. Sensing an advantage, I pressed
him for an explanation: how, in all those faces, could he spot a
Cambridge face? What was he talking about anyhow. What sort of
world was it in which Harris tweed defined allegiance? I couldn't
see the difference, and couldn't see that it made any difference,
and if he was just trying to scare me, well, he'd just better quit . . .

He dismissed the matter. Had he been a smoker, he would have
lit his pipe . . . "You'll see," he said. "You'll learn."

What we were asked to see and learn in college was considerable.
I studied hard, and by the time I was a junior I, too, could spot the
Cambridge face in a crowd full of hurrying strangers. That I was
wrong goes without saying; the face is various. Nor do I mean to
scold my brother, who is a compassionate man. But as I think back
on that tableau, I think I see how thoroughly we missed the point.
It is the sidelong glance that counts, the vista unannounced as such,
the presence in the corner of the eye.

"What Harvard has meant to me" means something very different now from what it seemed to mean. It is a certain way the shadow of the Fogg Museum bulks beneath the moon, a whiff of air in Widener in a section of the stacks, girls with book bags, argument, a ride on someone's motorcycle for the sheer sake of motion. It's a phrase like "parietal hours" or "Special, heavy on the dressing," that must seem code to anyone not locked within those walls those years, or escaped to Elsie's for a snack. It is admiration, imitation, and the high-hearted shock of knowing a professor knows your name. It is the wet chill of winter, brick buildings scarfed with snow, the Loeb at night or Charles river at dawn — the sense of endless possibility, of everything still left to learn, of all the world attendant on our youth.

I miss it and I honor it. It lasts. We are shapeshifters, and memory's a magic screen, and what we look like now or look for now is likely to be different. Last week I gave a talk in Virginia. Then I rented a car and drove to North Carolina. I was visiting a dear Harvard friend, a writer who had graduated one year earlier than I. He invited a third writer, one year my junior, who teaches now at Chapel Hill. It was hot; we sat outside. We made conversation. There were dogs and children everywhere; chickens scrabbled in the dirt. We could smell the supper cooking, hear the River Haw beneath us, and the bourbon was first-rate.

My colleagues leaned back in their chairs. One of them had thickened, one thinned. One had grown a moustache and one had shaved his off. We spoke of mutual acquaintances, of places we'd been or were going, of why who'd done what when. It started to rain. Geese honked; the children advanced on the porch. The marvellous woman my friend married announced we ought to eat. I had a moment, rising, when I knew what Harvard meant to me: reunion. Things fit. We were strangers subject to nostalgia and would be soon again; we were crossing a street with the light.

Nicholas Delbanco '63 is the author of nine novels. He teaches at Bennington College, and lives with his wife and two daughters in Vermont.

My Inadvertent Education
at Harvard

Unfortunately for my hope of uncovering fond memories, my years in Cambridge coincided with my adolescence — an adolescent torpor followed by a brief adolescent rage.

Life at Radcliffe in 1959 when I entered had not changed much in recent years. At 12:50 each Saturday night was a traffic jam of clinching couples on the Cabot Hall steps, while inside, girls in bathrobes and curlers waited out the shame of being dateless. We took turns at "bells", answering the single phone line, and taking down the pink messages from "Mr. X". These invariably brought shrieks of delight, and some of the girls collected them by the dozen as badges of popularity. I listened to lectures by great men about great men, and struggled to stay awake in a big chair in the Radcliffe library while reading the great men's words from page one to page 583. ("Let's see . . . at 43 pages an hour, it will take me until . . .")

By 1964, my senior year, the world of *in loco parentis* had fallen apart. Women checked out of Gilman house (the sprawling Victorian off-campus house where I lived for my last two years) for months at a time to stay with their boyfriends. The avant-garde at Harvard had begun to question the smug political wisdom of the '50s. A group called Tocsin organized protest marches against the arms race. A few students wrote and demonstrated in sympathy for the Vietcong. Others came back from sit-ins and freedom marches in the South. My friends and I were curious, but still too timid to participate.

My Inadvertent Education at Harvard

A *Crimson* article written by Faye Levine, a junior, helped explain us to ourselves. Called *The Three Flavors of Radcliffe*, it put forth the preposterous claim that all Radcliffe girls were either peaches, limes, or chocolates. Peaches had gone to prep school (or wished they had), dated men in final clubs, studied in the Widener reading room, and aspired to marry prominent men. Limes studied comparative literature in the Widener stacks, and expected to be junior editors, or at least secretaries to junior editors. They wore their hair long, just revealing their exotic earrings dangling from pierced ears, and hitchhiked through Europe with their boyfriends. Chocolates wore sensible clothes and looked wettest when it rained. They worked hard at organic chemistry and planned to become professors, scientists, or physicians. I was a peach aspiring to be a lime who didn't realize that deep down inside she was a chocolate.

Luckily, I was saved by rage from leaving Cambridge as timidly as I came. Harvard led me to feminism, surely as effective a mobilizer of adolescent passion in my era as Vietnam or South Africa have been in others. My inspiration was Betty Friedan's *The Feminine Mystique* which, long after my roommate had gone to sleep, I read in the closet, weeping over the fate of housewives buried alive amid their washers and freezers.

It was easy to work up a feminist rage at Harvard in 1964. Men lived in Houses with Masters and Senior Tutors; women lived in halls with sad, middle-aged housemothers. Men played squash; women took body mechanics in the rundown Radcliffe gym. Men delivered themselves of pompous appraisals of the cultural giants of the Western world; their girlfriends smiled appreciatively and learned to ask interesting questions. (Men were the admired editors of the *Crimson*; women were tolerated as reporters especially if they had *Crimson* boyfriends.)

Feminism gave me my first reason to think and speak for myself, and I made reluctant and irritated audiences of family, housemates and boyfriends for an entire year. But it also caused me to look again at history, economics, sociology — all I had studied — and was the beginning of my real education.

Harvard supplied only the first half of my personal education. The second half came from Rio de Janeiro, where I went right after graduation to work as an assistant cultural officer in the American Embassy. Harvard's fascination with comparative intellect and creative weirdness was filed away in favor of Rio's fascination with physical beauty and the creativity of a charmingly seductive con game. Where at Harvard I had studied distant worlds of Renaissance and Islamic history, in Rio I gobbled American history to understand who I was, and spent hours arguing politics and economics with the whiskey-drinking left. Harvard allowed me to define what my education should be; it was not until Rio that I actually undertook to educate myself.

My four years at Harvard were *not* the four best years of my life. But, in an odd way, the fierceness of my reaction to the closeness and smugness of that small world was an important part of my education. For those who fear they wasted their years in Cambridge as observers, Harvard's contribution may have been not so much to nurture them as to propell them outwards to seek their places in a larger world.

Mary Proctor '63 is a management consultant and former member of the Harvard Board of Overseers.

HEATHER DUBROW

On First Looking Into Sandy's Ovid

One day this fall, as I waited in Houghton Library for my books, I recalled reverently touching a 17th-century binding when I sat in the same reading room during my first term at Harvard. It is a measure of the excitement I experienced on that occasion some 20 years ago that I can even remember the volume I was reading: Sandy's edition of Ovid's *Metamorphoses*. I like to think that the teacher who directed me to it did so in part because he recognized that the antiquarian's delight in old books is not the least motivation behind a commitment to the life of the mind, that the aesthetic pleasure of handling such books is subtly but significantly related to the intellectual pleasure of reading them.

In any event, I now regret that though my Carleton students enjoy certain advantages that their Harvard counterparts might well envy, notably the predominance of small classes, they are denied the special sense of respect that comes from working with rare books while an undergraduate — respect for scholarship and for oneself as a potential scholar.

During that same first term at Harvard, I also learned a more painful but no less pertinent lesson about the life of the mind. My first English hour exam was returned with — horror of horrors — a B rather than an A and a comment I can still quote exactly: "Too much material canned from lectures." My initial reaction was astonishment; I was being criticized for what I had assumed was one of the principal virtues of my exam answers. Although I had attended an elite high school that emphasized independent thought,

I was sufficiently impressed at Harvard with the intellectual stature of the Great Man at the front of the lecture hall (an impression conveniently aided by the illusion of physical stature that a lecture stage provides) to believe that I should faithfully cast back the pearls that had been cast before me.

Recalling my subsequent undergraduate years, I can trace many other ways the University sparked and fostered intellectual excitement. I suspect, for example, that the very fact that three of my four tutors were in the Renaissance encouraged me to specialize in that field myself, and I am sure that my experiences reading Shakespeare's sonnets in junior and senior tutorial lie behind my current book on Shakespeare's nondramatic poetry. I am still grateful to the tutorial system that permitted me to work with such exciting and excited young faculty members early in my career.

On the other hand, I am less grateful about certain aspects of the educational milieu. At that point Harvard depended heavily on lecture courses that were supplemented neither with sections nor with essay assignments — courses that, therefore, implicitly encouraged the rote learning that my grader criticized. And I am aware that in my nine years as an undergraduate and graduate student at Harvard, I was taught by exactly one woman, a Teaching Fellow in *English 70*.

Like the structure of those Harvard lecture courses, the demographics of the Harvard faculty has changed significantly since I was an undergraduate. In most disciplines, female undergraduates now have the role models they need, and some of the blatant forms of prejudice that existed in the '60s and amaze students when I describe them today have now disappeared, ("You really weren't allowed in Lamont?" "You must be kidding—no female announcers on WHRB because women's voices were considered distracting?") Returning to Harvard in 1983, I found my reactions fluctuating between awareness of the changes that have occurred and an equally intense awareness of how many problems remain: is the glass half empty or half full?

My intellectual development was not without its outward and visible signs. Although I had not yet heard of semiotics, I eagerly latched onto mannerisms that could exemplify that science of signs: inch by inch both my hair and my earrings lengthened in the course of my four undergraduate years. I was, in brief, gradually trading my Manhattan psuedo-sophistication for Cambridge artiness. In fact, I still occasionally have nightmares that my hair has been cut against my will. *Pace* the traditional Freudians among my readers, I am sure that the primary significance of these hair-raising dreams is intellectual; I associate the increasing length of my hair with my increasing commitment to academics and to the Cantabridgian lifestyle with which I associated academics.

If I was changing between 1962 and 1966, Harvard was changing as well. The social and political conservatism of the '50s was still in evidence; Radcliffe women ritualistically donned pearl earrings for equally ritualistic Saturday-night dates, and one might even discover that, as it were, some of one's best friends were Republicans. But the mood of Cambridge was showing sings of shifting towards that of the Age of Aquarius.

It is as dangerous as it is tempting to generalize about shifts in undergraduate manners and mores. Nonetheless, one can safely say that students of my generation were beginning to react against the attitudes of the '50s, but the forms that reaction took were generally milder than those involving our younger brothers and sisters in the late '60s and early '70s. For in my day, unlike five years later, undergraduates variously participated in the Cambridge counterculture by leaving school temporarily to become civil rights workers rather than leaving permanently to become factory workers; by growing sideburns rather than growing beards; by dropping student government rather than dropping acid.

Some of my best memories are of the *Crimson*; the experience in writing, the close friends I made there, the interest in educational policy that still informs my career today. Yet if, as the saying goes, I had it to do over again, I would spend less time in that 14 Plympton Street fraternity. If the *Crimson* reflects some of what is best about Harvard, it also strikes me in certain ways as a microcosm of what is most dangerous about being an undergraduate here: the self-centered and self-satisfied parochialism.

I remember, for example, our congratulating ourselves on the fact that Jack Kennedy perused Cambridge's only breakfast daily and we trusted, profited from our judicious editorials. Some of my other regrets about my college years are connected with different but related types of parochialism that Cambridge fosters. I wish, for example, that I had spent more time in Boston. (The University could encourage students to do so — how about trips there during Freshman Week? More House activities in Boston?)

And then there are the memories of intense moments. I remember the way the bricks on the street shone in the rain as I walked back to Radcliffe; the way cups of hot cider and coffee steamed in a long defunct coffeehouse on a street whose name itself is now defunct, the Jolly Beaver of Boylston Street; the way the lilacs by Lamont smelled in spring. Nor have I forgotten the staler food smells in the Bick and Albiani's, all-night restaurants as sleazy as Boston politics. I can still recall how crisp and weighty the course catalogue felt as I sat under the trees in the yard to thumb through it. And I can recall the feel of that first of the many 17th-century books I've read in Houghton.

Heather Dubrow '66 received her Ph.D. in 1972 from Harvard; she also returned here as a Mellon Fellow in 1979-80 and as a Visiting Scholar in 1983-84. Associate Professor of English at Carleton College, she is the author of Genre *(Methuen) and of a number of articles on 16th- and 17th-century English literature; she is currently completing a book on Shakespeare's major non-dramatic poetry.*

Separate, Inseparable Worlds

Last summer, I walked up to introduce myself to a new summer intern in my office, a young woman who, I had been told, was attending a familiar institution in Cambridge. "I hear you're at Radcliffe," I said innocently. "I went there, too."

"Oh, did you call it Radcliffe?" was the breezy reply. "To us, it's all Harvard now."

That curt dismissal of a not-very-distant past still rankles a year later. Yes, dear, there really was a time when Harvard merely tolerated its modest quota of women, a time when we were welcomed unreservedly in only one small corner of that grand universe. And, yes, we did call it Radcliffe.

Not that we accepted the welcome without ambivalence. The pull of the male world was strong. There seemed a freedom and spontaneity to life at Harvard that Radcliffe lacked; our "gracious dining," back in the dorm, 6 p.m. sharp, dresses on, skirts required, was more constraint than grace. From the beginning, the magnet for me was the *Crimson*, my nest in the shadow of Adams House. But when the real shadows fell, the male *Crimson* editors repaired *en masse* to the all-male Adams House dining room before returning to our common enterprise of putting out the paper. For me, the long round-trip walk to Radcliffe was an unwelcome intrusion in a Harvard-centered day, so dinner was likely to be a solitary hamburger in the Square.

I don't mean to suggest that any of us were preoccupied with the status of women at Harvard, or even that we gave it much thought. It is mostly in retrospect that I see it in any particular relief. Then, it was simply part of the fabric of life, one thread among many.

True, when I think back to the first week of college, I vividly recall the mingled sense of thrill and horror with which I watched my fellow students file into the first section meeting of *Government 1-a*. All of them were men, all 30 of them. It was a high school girl's dream (I had turned down Smith, hadn't I?) and I wasn't sure why it felt more weird than wonderful.

But that was an extreme. In most of my other memories, Harvard and Radcliffe merge seamlessly, the ragged edges irrelevant. My most precious academic memory of that first year, if not of all four, is *Nat Sci 5*, George Wald's biology course, a broth of the life sciences so rich that a nonscientist like me could plunge in head first and still never quite drown. I'm more than a little hazy on the double helix these days, but that course conveyed a sense of wonder about the natural world that still resonates as powerfully as any great book or famous idea encountered on the more familiar terrain of literature or social science.

It was only after freshman year, my byline safely in place on the *Crimson* masthead, that I began to look around Radcliffe and value what I found there as something more than second-best to Harvard. Hilles Library opened, and it was so beautiful, so inviting, so much better than anything at Harvard that I think we all felt rather special simply because it was there. Harvard men flocked to Hilles, of course; so much the better, but it was ours. (All of a sudden, Harvard decided that our presence in Lamont Library would not, after all, create an unfavorable learning environment for the young men, but now no one was interested in using Lamont.)

It was also at about that time that the world's least willing athlete discovered the Radcliffe gym, suddenly deciding, after never having been closer to a horse than the clubhouse at Suffolk Downs, that I wanted to learn how to ride. The gym ferried us out to a stable in Jamaica Plain, and two years of weekly lessons served to increase my respect for horses much more than my mastery of them.

Separate, Inseparable Worlds

These were the waning peaceful years before the turmoil of the late 1960s came home to Harvard; in polite, formal sessions of student-faculty committees, we discussed the big issues such as whether to abolish the foreign language requirement or whether to expand opportunities for off-campus living. The latter was of no interest to me, as I figured I would have enough time after college to cook my own meals and pick up after myself; I think that was my one insight into the "real world" that proved to be valid.

It was over in a flash — my *Crimson* friends off on their travelling fellowships, still men-only in those days, and I off to work at what first seemed like a grand lark and only gradually solidified into something I'm not sure I had really expected, a career. I was ready and willing to leave Cambridge when the time came. Nostalgia came later, nostalgia for that awkward institutional amalgam of two worlds at once separate and inseparable. How to sort it all out? Oh, well, it's all Harvard now.

Linda Greenhouse '68 covers the Supreme Court for the New York Times *in their Washington Bureau. She is a former* Harvard Crimson *editor.*

DEBORAH TRUSTMAN

Learning about Love at Harvard

The first time I ever saw Harvard, I entered the Yard through the Johnson Gate. I felt as if I were coming into a shrine: the physical manifestation of the Harvard catalogue. I loved that fat red catalogue, passionately, for its secrets.

I was in Cambridge for an interview. It was Indian summer, the light that afternoon was golden, the grass was golden green, the leaves were beginning to turn, and after the noise of the Square, the Yard was quiet. I remember that the interior of Widener Library that day, was golden, too. As I started up the wide stairs to the reading room, I heard somebody above me whistling the slow movement of Brahms' *Fourth Symphony*. The sound echoed and amplified in the marble stairwell, and I was ravished. This was a place where music was the stuff of ordinary life; I could belong here. I loved it; I wanted it, hopelessly, I thought, to belong to me.

I did get accepted, and I came to Radcliffe looking for love of all kinds: intellectual passion, friendship, and sex. All I knew was infatuation. My career was painful, given my disastrous determination that every experience be transcendent, and given the time I was in college, which was the late '60s.

I spent my first year trying to adjust what I used to think of myself to the different standards of this place. I encountered an all gray New England boiled dinner for the first time. Coming from a Jewish high school on Long Island, I thought I had blond hair; when I got to Radcliffe, I saw I was wrong. I thought I knew a lot of music, and then I met another freshman who knew all 48 of Bach's preludes and figures by heart.

I waited to be swept away by knowledge, though I was afraid to take some courses and disappointed in others. I wanted magic, and I wasn't finding it. When I got A's I thought the college had made a mistake. The faculty's laissez faire attitude toward students — professors waiting to be approached — was hard on me; I didn't know enough to ask questions.

Revolutions, sexual and political, were rampant. During the years I was an undergraduate, rules and expectations — everything — changed. In 1964, we were required to wear skirts to supper, which was served to us (we took turns being "wait ons"). By 1969, we wore jeans and protest armbands in the cafeteria lines, and that spring, students occupied University Hall. It had become a privilege to teach us, a privilege which we, as students, could withdraw.

One friend engaged in pillow fights with her fiance instead of sex, and the first time I met her, another described how she was awakened that morning to find her lover painting her back. One night a girl in my dormitory ran naked up and down the halls and proclaimed her loss of virginity, not knowing whether she had been freed or trapped.

I'm not sure many of us knew; it was easier to say yes than no, and though love was more difficult than revolution, the act of love was not. We were activists; we did. We had discovered that nobody could stop us from doing anything, politically or personally.

When I fell in love, I felt delivered from the demands of liberation. I fell in love in terms of poetry. It was in spring, in time for the lilacs. He recited Keats to me, and I read Yeats to him; he played his guitar and taught me harmonies. At Sunday lunches at Adams House, we guessed which girls had spent Saturday night in which boys' rooms. When we ran out of poems and songs, we frightened each other. That fall, I went to Europe, drugs came to Cambridge, and he fell in love with marijuana.

When I came back, he'd graduated, and I retreated to the passion for learning — what I'd come to Harvard for in the beginning.

After a year in Rome trying to write and looking at great art, I decided to concentrate in Fine Arts; I loved paintings and knew something about them, and I didn't think I could write. The first thing that happened was that I learned how little I really did know, without becoming disillusioned. The second thing was that I learned how to see, which was the beginning of learning to write, although I didn't figure that out for years.

The department was small, elegant, and out of time: art was studied for its own sake. I memorized an enormous number of works of art, and to this day I sound like a tour guide when I tell you what Renaissance paintings are in what museum, or palace or church. To me, Fine Arts was a luxury, and a lucky break. Sidney Freedberg was my tutor. At our first meeting, he sat at his desk wearing a brown suit and a pale yellow vest with a shawl collar. He said hello to me in his resonant drawl, leaned back in his chair, and took snuff.

I watched, coolly I prayed, though I was so astonished that I couldn't move. I had read about snuff, but I had about never seen it. Professor Freedberg sneezed and showed me a picture. What was it? An aqueduct crossed the plain of the Roman campagna. It was Italian, of course. No, it was painted by an American in Italy. Look at the bright colors, the enthusiastic brush strokes. How is a painting put together? Look at the Titian, *The Rape of Europa*, in the Gardner Museum: the spirals, the pinwheel of red and blue in Europa's dress.

Professor Freedberg loved what he taught; he combined erudition with sensibility and humor; in one final exam, all the paintings we were to discuss had erotic subjects. For three hours we gazed at slides of voluptuous Venuses and Ledas and wrote about the anatomical distortions of mannerism.

I began to learn to look without prejudice; to clear my eyes and see not what *ought* to be there, but what actually *is* there. I began to see how things work: not only art, anything. More important,

196

Learning about Love at Harvard

I began to know how much greater love and mystery there can be with understanding. Understanding is a slow process; intuition and infatuation are only the first, heady steps. The rest is work. I began to learn understanding from looking at pictures, from a teacher who could communicate both his enthusiasm and his method. It is a lesson useful not only for art or writing books, but for life: it is the lesson in love I needed to learn.

Deborah Trustman '68 has written about the arts for many publications, including The Atlantic Monthly and The New York Times. Her first novel, about a journalist and a dancer, will be published next year.

THE BOK YEARS

1971 –

LEE A. DANIELS
Conflict in a Fervent Allegiance

I'm not a determinist, but since April, 1967, I have adhered to the supposition that my admission to Harvard was kismet. Some of the evidence:

During part of my childhood in Chicago, I lived on West 66th Street between Harvard and Yale Streets. Harvard Street was the quickest route to my elementary school.

My best friend in high school (we also lived directly across the street from each other) was a double Harvard "legacy" — his parents, respectively, were Harvard and Radcliffe graduates. From the moment we met, when we were 10 years old, Scott made it clear that Harvard was the college he would be attending.

Finally, at the awards ceremony during my junior year at the Boston Latin School — founded, I often make a point of noting, one year before Harvard itself — Wilfred O'Leary, its wonderful headmaster, quickly resolved my deliberations about college attendance by asking, mock-solemnly, "Lee, you do want to attend Harvard, don't you?" It was evident the question was rhetorical. My mother's face shone with the radiance of a lighthouse beacon, and I was on my way to Harvard.

I soon discovered several reasons for the fervent allegiance to Harvard I so swiftly developed: my respect for intellectual distinction, inculcated in the most subtle ways by my parents; my reverence for tradition and history because they offered a means of placing myself in context, if you will, and of searching out where I came from and what my role in life was to be; my quest for achievement, in order to prove to the world and to myself that I was "special"; and my attraction to the trappings of elitism, of which, of course, Harvard had no lack.

From that September Friday morning in 1967 when I rushed from Boston to Cambridge to be in the Yard shortly after the freshman dorms opened for the school year, I was enthralled with Harvard — more, much more at first by its ambiance of deserved and easily assumed privilege and its pageantry than by its intellectual substance. Even then I noticed and was impressed by the intellectual assertiveness and brilliance of many of my classmates. It was the first time in my life I had encountered people my own age who were as bright as I was — or even brighter.

Although I appreciated Harvard's general tone of intellectual skepticism, I didn't really have a deep interest in its academic side; instead, I was obsessed with adding to my resume those "prestigious" activities which look so good in the yearbook. However, through the efforts of such people as Martin Kilson and Doris Kearns and Florence Ladd and David Riesman, my intellectual curiosity did awaken and flower. They were most responsible for my leaving Harvard aware that I had a lifetime of learning ahead of me and being eager for it.

I'm sure that to some who knew me, my fundamental comfort with Harvard, especially during that period of broad social turmoil, must have seemed a striking incongruity in one who had grown up in black ghettos and who was as aware as I was of Harvard's and America's checkered racial past. But if I then dimly perceived that the sum of my feelings about both added up to a contradiction, I also intuitively realized that Harvard was the best place for me to come to grips with racism in America — what better place to compete against the best white society had to offer, and to learn, as I did, that, despite my acute and growing race-related bitterness, there were some whites I could treasure as close friends after all.

Throughout those exciting, fractious, necessary years of protest at Harvard, I did not, I am proud to say, let my love for Harvard prevent me from bearing witness, if only in a minor way, to its ignorance and myopia about some things. Yet, at the same time, my basic feeling about Harvard never wavered. (If that remains a contradiction, so be it.) Not until I graduated did I fully understand that my activism there represented, not a reversal of my earlier feelings, but a ripening of a naive infatuation into a critical but abiding affection. In the years since, I've grown to appreciate ever more deeply the opportunity of attending Harvard, and, as I remain committed to the social causes I supported then, so too I remain committed to Harvard, dear Alma Mater.

Lee Daniels '71 is a staff reporter for the New York Times.

ANDREA LEE

Possessed of Wings

I came to Harvard in the fall of 1970, when Harvard Square was still an outpost of Never Never Land, a stopover for ragtag children of the Aquarian Age on their journey toward revolution or Nirvana; a mob of Hari Krishnas danced daily in front of Holyoke Center and in the Yard, people nonchalantly predicted spring riots as if they were speaking of spring rain. On the Sunday that my parents drove me into Cambridge, the Common was crammed with students and street people smoking joints and making unabashed love on blankets as they listened to a series of rock bands; on Garden Street, at least 20 motorcycles were revving up under the heels of what looked like Hell's Angels.

"Oh, dear," said my mother faintly, as she passed the motorcyclists. She repeated "Oh, dear" in a still fainter voice when we entered Currier House and she met the cheerful young man moving into the room across the hall from mine. Nothing alarmed me: I was thrilled at the sight of the youth carnival I was joining, and, as soon as I decently could, I set my parents on the road back to Philadelphia. When they were gone, I mounted my bicycle and plunged into the traffic of Mass. Ave. to explore my new world. I can recall exactly the blissful sensation of absolute freedom I experienced on that ride, as I wove through the Common, zipped into the Yard to gape at Widener, zigzagged between the River Houses, and finally raced up Memorial Drive. I felt possessed of wings; it seemed that a whole new dimension of liberty and license was open to me.

Freedom was indeed what I had at Harvard, a moral and academic independence, delightful to a 17-year-old fresh from the confines of a strict girls' school. At that time, Harvard had so recently discarded so many traditions that in parts of student life blank spots existed where there were no precedents for behavior and a sort of anarchy prevailed. For someone like me, adept at sidling past regulations, it was a place in which — sometimes fortunately and sometimes disastrously — I found my way. I embarked immediately upon a tumultuous romance, and academic life became equally tumultuous since my choice of courses was dictated largely by whim. Somehow, through the vast muddle of my studies it became clear to me that English Literature was my great love, and suddenly I had a path to follow. Majoring in English meant a series of breathless crushes on dead and living poets and on the professors who taught their work; writing papers was an act of devotion marked by periods of suicidal despondency on the third floor of Hilles and mournful orgies of chocolate chip cookies. As a sophomore, I wandered into William Alfred's course in Anglo-Saxon literature and ended up staying on to translate *Beowulf*. That same year, I was accepted into a division of the English major that allowed me to concentrate on writing fiction and poetry. I worked with Francine Prose, who impressed me with her calm dedication to writing, and with Robert Fitzgerald, for whom I felt such a suffocating awe that spots danced in front of my eyes whenever I faced him.

At Commencement 1974, I emerged into the world not particularly wise or knowledgeable but aware, at least, of what direction I wanted to take. Many of my friends at other colleges had been guided through courses and social life with a thoroughness that, at certain points, became control; I moved through Harvard in a blissful chaos, avoiding a series of advisors, guided mainly by my own instincts — instincts that occasionally got me into trouble. Quite often I yearned for a bustling House mother or a stern tutor to lay down the law for me. Mostly, though, I took a stiff-necked pride in my own independence. Often on my bike, I repeated the ride I had taken during my first few hours at Harvard. Each time, as I darted up Memorial Drive between the brick walls, the syca- mores, and the river, I had the glorious feeling of being under my own power and on my way somewhere.

Andrea Lee '74, MA '78, is a staff writer for The New Yorker and author of Russian Journal *(1981). She is currently completing a novel.*

D A V I D   U P D I K E

What They Never Told Me About Harvard

My Harvard transcript records a mixed academic history — a dabbling in the arts and sciences with an emphasis on mediocrity. My method for success, unlike my peers, was to attend all of my classes, read all books, write all papers, and take all tests in the comforting knowledge that I had done all that was asked of me, and was obliged to do no more; through diligence, I excused myself from the more strenuous pursuit of excellence.

This formula was succesful until my junior year when, for reasons never quite clear to me, I enrolled in *Biology 103*. Although I loved *The Taxonomy of Seed-Bearing Plants*, it was more for esthetic reasons that botanical ones: I loved the fantastic, looming shapes of flowers as seen through the high-powered microscope; I enjoyed the field trips we took to the Arnold Arboretum where, like a flock of ducklings we followed our instructor from shrub to tree; the weekly slide shows of the world's flora, as much as I now love knowing that the hoary redness of trees in spring is caused by the blooming of their million, miniscule flowers; that apples, peaches, and cherries are siblings, and cousins of the rose; that certain pine cones are designed to open and release their seeds only in the event of fire.

My downfall came with the first test, and the blur of these happy observations dissolved before the sudden, desperate need of scientific facts: flowers could, and must, be identified by a simple row of numbers, denoting petals, sepals, tepals; the dandelion's puff, or the apple's spiraling seed, is a "mechanism of dispersal"; the fruit of *Canabis stativa* (the only plant I had ever farmed), was an "achene." I knew, after an unpleasant hour, that I had met my match, and soon thereafter dropped the course. But the deadline had already passed and so one of my favorite courses also became the only one, in 16 years of formal education, that I officially failed.

My strongest courses were those generally dismissed as "guts"; *The History of the American Landscape* ("Gas Stations"), *The Great Age of Discovery* ("Boats"); *Astronomy* 8. Each of these seemed closer to reality to me — a direct, tangible description of the physical world. That was generally avoided in academia. Knowledge was delivered in fascinating, mind-boggling facts: if a Harvard student fell into a black hole, for example, he, or she, would instantly be reduced to the size of a proton.

My happiest memories of Harvard, though, are not academic ones. Each of my four years comes to me now as a discreet, independent packet: Freshman year I spent in the company of my four roommates, looking out our window in Weld. I attended an occasional party, pursued an occasional girl, but generally was happy to go about my business, attend my classes, and play for the triumphant freshman soccer team.

As a sophomore, I moved with a friend to Winthrop House, across the hall from a suite of five attractive girls. I spent most waking hours in their room, most sleeping hours in mine, and by the Yale game, had fallen hopelessly in love. I spent the next 12 months in a state of suspended unhappiness, highlighted only by shimmering sparks of euphoria, in which all other objects and people were stage props, distractions from what consumed and colored my world.

Together, we thrashed through an unimagined forest of words and feelings, varieties and definitions of love, from which I miraculously emerged, intact, a year later. I was older, wizened, a certain kind of innocence lost forever.

Junior year I regressed, and spent most evenings playing "nerf soccer" in my room, the empty fireplace for one goal, the doorway for another, my roommate and several friends for players and spectators. Now and then the neighboring pre-med would appear for a good natured plea for quiet and, after a moment of respectful deliberation, the game would furiously resume.

By senior year I had moved off campus, I had a new girlfriend, a bicycle, and took great pleasure in hurtling down Mass. Ave. between her house and mine at all hours of the night and day, hair blowing in the wind. The future did not worry me much. By that time I had begun to write and imagined that, in one form or another, I would continue.

Excepting several seasons of malaise, my years at Harvard were very happy ones. In the years since graduation, my only regret is that I was not better warned for what was to follow. In retrospect it seems to me that my parents and teachers were all keepers of an enormous secret, and neglected to tell me that my days were numbered, that their gift of four years would end, and that this, my college life, would bear little resemblance to what lay beyond. I did not then know that I would suddenly be required to be something rather than someone, or that the problems of real life are both simpler, and less easy to solve, than those I had become familiar with. Nobody ever told me, as someone once said, "The greatest lesson of a college education is how little it will avail you." I had to learn it myself.

David Updike '79 is a short story writer who contributes to The New Yorker magazine.

DAVID E. SANGER

Harvard and the Real World

It has been a year now since the bagpiper awakened us from the courtyard of Lowell House, and then led us, like the Pied Piper, into the Yard for Commencement. We were being delivered to that long-feared moment that would mark our exit into the "real world," the catch-phrase parents and Commencement speakers used to characterize everything beyond the protected enclave in which we had lived for four years. The unspoken implication of the term is that everything had been easy thus far, and if you really want to see how tough things can get, just wait a while.

A year in the real world is insufficient time to determine if they were right. Even 20 years may not do it. But a year is enough time to compare what I expected in 1978 to get out of Harvard and what I actually left with in 1982. Strikingly, there is not much similarity between the two.

I'm still not sure why I went to Harvard. At the time, it seemed the right thing to do. I was drawn by the prestige of the place, the reputation of the teaching staff, the revered place it holds — deservedly or not — in American folklore. I expected a lot of hard work, of course. Unconsciously, though, I think I came to Cambridge expecting to be something of the passive actor in the whole process. I would enter. Harvard would do its thing to me, and I would leave a different person.

I did leave a different person, but it didn't happen quite the way I expected. Harvard, I learned, is not a place for passivity. It is a place for making difficult choices. The choices themselves don't seem so terribly weighty now; which courses to take, whether or not to write a thesis, what kinds of activities to jam between academics. What makes Harvard such a place for self-discovery, though, is the fact that it leaves so many of those choices to its students. And then, to make it all the more challenging, it adds thousands of distractions and opportunities. Most of them passed me by, and sometimes I regret missing as many as I did. But I am consoled by the fact that Harvard taught me how to choose and learning how to do that may be as important as the choices I ultimately made.

The point is that at Harvard education became a very active, a very participatory thing. And while I sometimes felt cast adrift at sea in what the *Crimson* once called Harvard's "have-a-cookie" approach to making discriminating choices, the system also taught me something about freedom. Not the kind of freedom we learned about in *Gov. 10*, but the difference between free time and unstructured time, and the role of each in encouraging creativity.

Free time is scarce in Cambridge, at least if you are not letting too many of the opportunities slip by. But as a student I had a lot of unstructured time, and the biggest challenge I faced was learning how to structure it most effectively. By unstructured time, I mean time in which to exercise those choices that I made for myself. Deciding how to structure one's time, I quickly learned was the same as deciding how to channel one's most creative energies. Today I miss that kind of freedom the most, for one great disadvantage of the much-heralded "real world" is the degree to which others structure your time for you. As a result, I have more free time, but less unstructured time, and more of it is probably wasted.

A year away from Cambridge has also made me more conscious than ever before of Harvard's split personality. Every graduate has two images of the place, I suspect, and they differ a fair amount. One of them is a very personal image, a Harvard that centers around the people we lived with, the professors we knew, and the greasy fries in Tommy's Lunch at two o'clock in the morning. That is the Harvard I feel when I walk around in the Yard these days. Somehow, those walks remind me of standing in a giant, empty stadium about a half hour after the game is over. The fans are gone, and the players have retired to the locker room. What remains is a ringing in my ears, the memory of the background noise that accompanied the great plays. Still, it is just an echo, and it will never be quite the same again.

The other Harvard, the institutional Harvard, rarely changes, and about it I have more mixed emotions. And it has struck me, even more than it did as a student, that like any other major institution Harvard faces up to its symbolic responsibilities only at its convenience. When it uses its symbolic influence well, it can make powerful statements. For example, by extending an invitation to Lech Walesa to speak at this Commencement, Harvard not only made an important point about Mr. Walesa's role as a freedom fighter; it also openly challenged any remaining pretenses by the Polish government that it was not fearful of nonviolent dissent. By lending Harvard's name to the offer, even greater attention was focused on the values for which Mr. Walesa stands.

When dealing with internal matters, however, Harvard often seems to feign surprise when the outside world, particularly the media, finds important symbolism in its actions. The University's often faltering efforts to bring minorities and women into the faculty of some departments, or to confront its responsibilities as a significant shareholder in some corporations, are of symbolic importance equivalent to its encouragement of unfettered discussions about world policy. My point is that Harvard, like its students, cannot get away with not making choices.

Such criticism aside, though, a year away has deepened my respect for both Harvards, the personal one and the institutional one. Barely a day goes by when I do not long to be back in Cambridge, along with the people who meant so much to me there. How could anything so real, and anything so greatly missed, not be part of the real world?

David E. Sanger '82 was the Harvard College correspondent for The New York Times, until he graduated. He is now a news clerk in the Times business and financial section.

WILLIAM MCKIBBEN

Three Favorite Places

Perhaps because so many details slip away, memory becomes more meaningful as time passes. I am still much too close to my four years at Harvard to be able to say what they truly meant to me, to say they made me a man, or turned me old and cynical, or filled me with a love for learning. I am, as yet, able to remember only things — people and places, not passages. People are too difficult to write about. So I shall concentrate on three places at Harvard that meant a lot to me.

The first — and by far the most important — was the crumbling brick building at 14 Plympton St. that housed the *Crimson*, "Cambridge's Only Breakfast Table Daily." I know every inch of it by heart, for I spent a thousand nights in its company. I know where the stairs are loose, where the carpet is shredded, what closet holds a stash of *Crimson* neckties from the 1940s, where the water comes through the ceiling when it rains, dripping on the rolls of newsprint. I also know, however, that those who have never tried out for the *Crimson* have little wish to know more about it, and that they will dismiss my love as inexplicable infatuation. Anyway, my passion for the building was personal, and to talk too much about it seems almost profane.

Better to describe the other two places, both of them more or less public, and both discovered in the spring of my senior year when I finally had to leave the *Crimson* to other suitors. The first, Kirkland House Library, I kept a secret at the time, for solitude was chief among its charms. A pre-revolutionary white frame house, it rests at the isolated end of the Kirkland House annex; in its low-ceilinged, warp-floored rooms there are perhaps 10,000 books, and just the right 10,000 books. A narrow staircase wound up the center of building, and the best of the two rooms on the top floor contained the European history collection. One could close the door, settle into a soft chair, and spend an uninterrupted afternoon feeling like a student, or even like a scholar — like someone who took books and silences seriously.

The other place, Appleton Chapel, hardly needed to be hushed up — at least in my time at the College, the announcement that Michael Jackson was to read the New Testament lesson would not have swelled the crowd at morning prayers past its usual 20 familiar faces. Familiar though not intimate — each morning I tried to sit behind a soprano with a thrilling voice whom I have never met or talked to for that would have spoiled it.

The first day I went, some aging classicist spoke on the need to separate church and politics, citing "Render unto Caesar" as his source. It seemed bad policy and bad theology both, but I loved the hymn and so kept going; most mornings I emerged into the yard either humming some anthem or chewing on the sermonette just delivered, and on many happy mornings both.

Gradually I came to realize that my affection for morning prayers masked some genuine affection for the idea of Harvard, an affection that had largely been hidden over the years by my profound disgust with many of the University's policies — its stock portfolio, its callousness toward Cambridge, its conservatism and its cronyism. For 350 years, without fail, students and faculty had gathered in small numbers each morning; somehow that continuity made Harvard's current failings seem . . . not less important, but less eternally.

William McKibben '82 is a staff writer for The New Yorker magazine.